Disaster Stress Studies: New Methods and Findings

CLINICAL INSIGHTS

Disaster Stress Studies: New Methods and Findings

**Edited by
James H. Shore, M.D.**

*Professor and Chairman, Department of Psychiatry,
University of Colorado School of Medicine*

AMERICAN PSYCHIATRIC PRESS, INC.
Washington, D.C.

Copyright © 1986 American Psychiatric Press, Inc.

ALL RIGHTS RESERVED

Manufactured in the U.S.A.

The paper used in this publication meets the minimum requirements of American National Standard for Information Sciences—Permanence of Paper for Printed Library Materials, ANSI Z39.48-1984. ∞™

Library of Congress Cataloging in Publication Data

Main entry under title:

Disaster stress studies.

(Clinical insights)
Based on a symposium held in Dallas, Tex. at the Annual Meeting of the American Psychiatric Association in the spring of 1985.
Includes bibliographies.
1. Post-traumatic stress disorder—Congresses. 2. Disaster victims—Mental health—Congresses. 3. Disasters—Psychological aspects—Congresses. I. Shore, James H, 1940- . II. American Psychiatric Association. Meeting (138th : 1985 : Dallas, Tex.) III. Series [DNLM: 1. Data Collection—methods—congresses. 2. Disasters—congresses. 3. Stress Disorders, Post-Traumatic—congresses. WM 170 D6104 1985]
RC552.P67D53   1986   616.85'21   86-10913
ISBN 0-88048-133-1 (soft)

Contents

Contributors

EVELYN J. BROMET, PH.D.
Associate Professor of Psychiatry and Epidemiology, Western Psychiatric
Institute and Clinic, University of Pittsburgh

LINDA B. COTTLER, M.P.H.
Research Patient Coordinator—Professional, Department of Psychiatry,
Washington University School of Medicine, St. Louis, Missouri

RUTH L. FISCHBACH, PH.D.
Psychiatry Trainee, National Institute of Mental Health, Washington
University School of Medicine, St. Louis, Missouri

EVELYN GOLDRING, M.A.T.
Research Patient Coordinator—Professional, Department of Psychiatry,
Washington University School of Medicine, St. Louis, Missouri

MARDI J. HOROWITZ, M.D.
Professor of Psychiatry, Langley Porter Psychiatric Institute,
University of California, San Francisco

J. DAVID KINZIE, M.D.
Professor of Psychiatry, Oregon Health Sciences University, Portland

THOMAS R. PRZYBECK, PH.D.
Statistical Data Analyst, Department of Psychiatry, Washington University
School of Medicine, St. Louis, Missouri

LEE N. ROBINS, PH.D.
Professor of Sociology in Psychiatry, Washington University School of
Medicine, St. Louis, Missouri

HERBERT C. SCHULBERG, PH.D.
Professor of Psychiatry and Psychology, Western Psychiatric Institute and
Clinic, University of Pittsburgh

JAMES H. SHORE, M.D.
Professor and Chairman of Psychiatry, University of Colorado
School of Medicine, Denver

ELIZABETH M. SMITH, PH.D.
Assistant Professor of Psychiatry, Washington University
School of Medicine, St. Louis, Missouri

SUSAN D. SOLOMON, PH.D.
Emergency Research Coordinator, National Institute of Mental Health,
Rockville, Maryland

ELLIE L. TATUM, M.S.W.
Instructor of Psychiatry, Oregon Health Sciences University, Portland

WILLIAM M. VOLLMER, PH.D.
Assistant Professor of Psychiatry, Oregon Health
Sciences University, Portland

Introduction

For modern psychiatry few areas have attracted more interest than human response to massive collective stress, from both technological and natural disasters. A number of modern disasters have received careful study and have become bywords in our professional language. These include the Coconut Grove fire, the Buffalo Creek flood, and the Chowchilla kidnappings, which were contributed to our professional language by Lindemann (1944), Titchener and Kapp (1976), and Terr (1983). Other contributors like Lifton (1968), Frederick (1980), and Horowitz (1976) have given us insight into the long-term adjustment, differential reactions, and clinical aspects of stress response syndromes. From psychiatry's perspective there is no doubt that major disaster stress causes significant mental disorder, although some social scientists (Quarantelli 1979) have consistently challenged this viewpoint. Our field has advanced from clinical description to the development, in the post-Vietnam era, of a new diagnostic classification that includes posttraumatic stress disorder.

Two experiences have influenced my involvement in disaster research, one professional and one personal. My professional interest in psychiatric epidemiology began when I was assigned to the Indian Health Service, where I had the opportunity to plan rural mental health programs throughout the Pacific Northwest. This interest was reawakened by the significant advances in epidemiological methods that have occurred during the past decade. These advances began with more systematic diagnostic criteria, the *Diagnostic and Statistical Manual of Mental Disorders (Third Edition) (DSM-III;* American Psychiatric Association 1980), the Diagnostic Interview Schedule (DIS), and the epidemiology catchment area studies that applied these new techniques to address questions of community patterns and etiologies of psychiatric disorders. The personal factor in my interest in disaster research was that a volcano, Mount St. Helens, erupted 40 miles from my living room window—practically in my backyard. It is difficult to avoid the personal questions of disaster impact when you are sweeping volcanic ash from your patio.

As the plan for a systematic study of the Mount St. Helens disaster began, the interest of our project team (Ellie Tatum, William Vollmer, and myself) was focused on these new research techniques, which had not been applied extensively to the study of stress response syndromes. We were fortunate to collaborate with colleagues who had a similar interest and who were experts in these areas. Dr. Evelyn Bromet was studying the disaster response at Three Mile Island, Dr. Lee Robins was applying the DIS methodology in a follow-up at Times Beach, Missouri, and Dr. David Kinzie was adapting similar techniques to study the adjustments of Southeast Asian refugees. From these projects came the idea for a symposium on disaster stress studies and the new methods and findings that were emerging. This symposium took place at the annual meeting of the American Psychiatric Association, and it formed the basis for this monograph.

This monograph contains descriptions of four separate studies in which psychiatric disorders resulting from life-threatening stress were investigated. Three of these studies focused on the victims of the technological and natural disasters at Three Mile Island, Times Beach, and Mount St. Helens. The fourth focused on adolescent and adult refugees from Vietnam and Cambodia. In all of these studies, systematic diagnostic criteria were used with a community epidemiological method. The DIS was used for the first time following a major disaster in two of the four studies. The findings documented a differential occurrence of stress response disorders and varying patterns of psychiatric impairment. The impairment appears to be related to the nature and intensity of the disaster stress. For certain populations the findings substantiated significant psychiatric morbidity from disaster stress experience. Overall, the outcomes demonstrated the uniqueness of major stress experience and a differential effect on each population.

James H. Shore, M.D.

REFERENCES

Frederick CJ: Effects of natural vs. human-induced violence upon victims. Evaluation and Change, Special Issue: 71-75, 1980

Horowitz MJ: Stress Response Syndromes. New York, Jason Aronson, 1976

Lifton RJ: Death in Life—The Survivors of Hiroshima. London, Weidenfeld and Nicholson, 1968

Lindemann E: Symptomatology and management of acute grief. Am J Psychiatry 101:141-148, 1944

Quarantelli EL: The consequences of disasters for mental health: conflicting views. Preliminary Paper No. 62, Ohio State University, Columbus, 1979

Terr LC: Chowchilla revisited: the effects of psychic trauma four years after a school-bus kidnapping. Am J Psychiatry 140:1543-1550, 1983

Titchener JL, Kapp FT: Family and character change at Buffalo Creek. Am J Psychiatry 133:295–316, 1976

1

The Three Mile Island Disaster: A Search for High-Risk Groups

Evelyn J. Bromet, Ph.D.
Herbert C. Schulberg, Ph.D.

1

The Three Mile Island Disaster: A Search for High-Risk Groups

During the summer of 1979, the Disaster Assistance and Emergency Mental Health Section of the National Institute of Mental Health (NIMH) asked us to undertake an epidemiologic study of the mental health effects of the Three Mile Island (TMI) nuclear accident, which had occurred that March. We considered this investigation to be particularly challenging for both scientific and political reasons. First, TMI differed from any of the stressors studied previously by social scientists. Unlike other natural or technological disasters, which produce various types of damage, no lives or property was lost after the nuclear reactor failed. Also, unlike acute life events, the stressful duration of which is finite, serious problems at TMI persisted and unfolded over time. Thus, an appropriate conceptual framework that incorporated TMI's unique features was needed to guide data collection. Second, we knew of no prior psychiatric epidemiologic research on cataclysmic events. Earlier studies were either case reports or investigations

This research was supported by National Institute of Mental Health Grant MH35425 and funds from the W. T. Grant Foundation. We wish to thank Leslie Dunn, M.P.H., for coordinating the field work and Ben Locke, M.S., Chief, Center for Epidemiologic Studies, National Institute of Mental Health, for his encouragement and support throughout the planning and implementation of the project.

in which complex issues surrounding sample selection, control groups, standardized measurement procedures, and timing of data collection generally were not considered. Third, it was anticipated that legal suits would be filed for psychic distress, so we were concerned about designing a study, the findings of which might validly be used in complex court proceedings. Fourth, we wished to investigate diagnostic-level psychiatric outcomes instead of simply symptoms of distress, even though prior to the TMI study a diagnostic instrument (SADS-L) had only been used in one community study (Weissman and Myers 1978). Finally, the effects of a cataclysmic event can linger long after the event itself, so we needed to design a longitudinal study of several years duration despite the initial assurance of funding for only one year.

This chapter describes our approaches to these diverse conceptual and methodological challenges as we investigated the potential psychiatric effects of the TMI nuclear accident. The results of our research on affected groups have previously been reported in separate papers (Bromet and Dunn 1981; Bromet et al. 1982a, 1982b, 1984; Dew et al. 1985; Parkinson and Bromet 1983; Schulberg et al. 1984). They are integrated here for the first time to provide a cohesive picture of the accident's effects on differing high-risk populations.

CONCEPTUALIZING THE THREE MILE ISLAND ACCIDENT

The logical starting point for designing an investigation of the psychiatric sequelae of the TMI accident was the selection of a conceptual model causally linking exposure to outcome. Such a theoretic framework would provide a basis for all subsequent methodologic and analytic decisions. This strategy is hardly controversial, but, surprisingly, it has rarely been implemented in prior studies of a disaster's long-term effects. Because few researchers or clinicians have been able to and/or interested in following cohorts over extended time periods to ascertain the natural history of stress reactions, little is known about the dynamics of chronic as compared to acute stress. Pertinent conceptual models, therefore, were lacking for our long-term follow-up studies. We were aware of reports that the psychological consequences of exposure to a disaster extend beyond the disaster's initial phase (Kinston and Rosser 1974), but the literature was ambiguous about the persistence and nature of these sequelae. For example, Lifton (1967) and Hocking (1970) emphasized the detrimental impairment that results from exposure to cataclysmic events, whereas Quarantelli and Dynes (1973) noted the potentially positive consequences of such events. These opposing views may be attributable to the varying characteristics of disasters (for example, some disasters can be anticipated so that interventions can be planned, others cannot) or to methodological bias produced by studying persons who participate in rescue operations and benefit from the experience while omitting those distressed enough to leave the area.

Given the dearth of information about the dynamics and consequences of long-term stress, our starting point for developing a conceptual model was the existing knowledge base on the characteristics of acute stress and the diverse mechanisms through which it is manifested. In particular, we were drawn to the conceptual framework of B.P. Dohrenwend et al. (1982), which suggests that adjustment is mediated by situational and personal factors, and to the work of Lazarus et al. (1980), which emphasizes the need to distinguish the objective nature of a potentially stressful circumstance from a person's subjective appraisal of it. Moreover, we were also influenced by Janis (1962) who postulated that a person compromises between the need to remain ever vigilant and the quest for reassurance that the potential danger is no longer threatening. Within Janis's framework, maladaptive patterns are thought to develop when the perceived threat is so strong as to prevent compromise formations.

The conceptual model of chronic stress that we constructed for the TMI study was based on these earlier works, but it was also influenced by our own thoughts regarding variables that might be causally linked to long-term outcome. Specifically, we postulated that: 1) Most people cope with disasters or other life events without serious psychological difficulty or with only transitory symptoms. Nevertheless, population subgroups that were at greater risk for experiencing adverse psychological reactions to TMI could be identified. 2) As Fried (1982) subsequently confirmed, the most prevalent long-term consequence of chronic stress was likely to be affective disorder and associated symptomatology. 3) The most important personal factors that might increase the likelihood that an individual would suffer psychiatric illness were a prior psychiatric disorder, pregnancy at the time of the accident (among women), and the perception of TMI as dangerous. 4) The most significant situational factors that might influence the severity of psychiatric sequelae were living nearer to TMI and perceiving inadequate levels of social support from within and outside one's household. With regard to the value of social support systems, Caplan (1981) concluded from earlier research that high levels of social support protect against the vulnerability to illness that results from high stress. Persons who do not share such relationships lack vital interpersonal resources and are but marginal participants in community efforts to resolve a disaster's deleterious consequences. Our conceptual model, thus, was an amalgam of earlier research suggesting factors that directly or indirectly affect psychiatric outcome. The personal characteristics of prior psychiatric history and the situational factors of residential proximity to TMI and current social support level were conceptualized as particularly influential elements in the adjustment process.

DESIGNING THE STUDY

The first major design issue that confronted us was the choice of cohorts to be studied to determine TMI's long-term effects. We did not believe that a sample of all persons exposed to the accident should be followed because the prevalence of mental illness in untreated populations is known to be low (Weissman and Myers 1978). We also assumed that most people had effectively coped with the accident, adjusting to it with the same skills as they would use in other stressful events. Furthermore, the Behavioral Effects Task Force of the President's Commission on The Accident at Three Mile Island was examining short-term effects on selected high-risk groups (Dohrenwend et al. 1979, 1981); we wished to

compare our long-term findings with the more acute impact addressed by this task force. Our funding source (NIMH), however,
encouraged us to focus on a random sample of the entire community so our findings could be generalized to the affected population
as a whole. Fortunately, the monetary resources available for the
TMI study were limited. Consequently, resorting to both scientific and practical logic, we persuaded the NIMH that our ability
to detect significant effects would be enhanced by sampling from
selected high-risk groups rather than by studying the population at
large.

Having successfully advocated the merits of studying only high-
risk subpopulations, we must acknowledge the constraints im-
posed by this strategy. First, it is more difficult to compile a proper
sampling frame and to obtain the cooperation of needed participants in delimited cohorts than it is in door-to-door surveys. Second, with our strategy, the findings are necessarily limited to the
specific groups studied and cannot be generalized beyond them.

Given these scientific and practical concerns, we were able to
choose three high-risk cohorts that accommodated our conceptual,
fiscal, and political considerations. Our first high-risk group consisted of mothers of preschool children living within 10 miles of
the nuclear plant; the governor of Pennsylvania had singled out
those within five miles for evacuation immediately after the
accident. These women were concerned about the effects of possible exposure to radiation both on their own reproductive systems
and on their children's health. Earlier British studies (Brown and
Harris 1978; Moss and Plewis 1977; Richman 1974, 1977) have
suggested that mothers of preschool children are at high risk for
affective disorders and symptomatology if they experience life
threatening events. Our second high-risk group consisted of workers employed at the nuclear plant when the accident occurred.
They were most directly involved in the accident and considerable
anxiety was expressed about their physical safety as well as their
economic security should the facility remain closed. Also reports
had circulated (and were later confirmed) that the children of
these workers were being harassed in school by classmates and
teachers and that their wives were being ostracized by neighbors.

Because no data had been previously reported on the mental health status of nuclear power plant workers, scientific gains of a more general and immediate nature could be achieved by including this group in the study. The third high-risk group consisted of persons living within 10 miles of TMI who had recently received psychiatric treatment. This cohort, presumably vulnerable to the additional stress of exposure to a nuclear accident, was also of concern to NIMH. Surprisingly, few earlier studies had investigated even the short-term reactions of psychiatric inpatients and outpatients to natural or technological disasters. A further contribution of our research, therefore, was to extend the limited knowledge base concerning whether disaster-induced stress increases symptomatology in psychiatric patients.

The second major design issue to be resolved was the selection of a comparison site. A common limitation of disaster research is the investigator's inability to collect the baseline data needed to assess an event's true impact on the population being studied. One possible strategy for dealing with this crucial problem is to include a comparison group. However, most disaster studies, including the relatively sophisticated Buffalo Creek project (Gleser et al. 1981), did not include control groups of any sort. An investigator's failure to deal with this design issue produces serious problems when it comes time to interpret the findings. This is particularly true if the disaster occurs in an atypical location to which normative data from urban populations on the prevalence of mental illness and patterns of stress reactions may be inapplicable.

Our selection of valid comparison groups for TMI subjects was complicated because in the study's first year the level of funding permitted data collection at only one additional site when, ideally, two should have been used. Optimally, the first comparison group should consist of demographically similar persons potentially vulnerable to but not actually exposed to the stressful event; in this instance, people living near or working at another nuclear plant. The second comparison group ideally should consist of demographically similar persons not facing any potential threat of disaster. For the first year of our study, during which time two face-to-face interviews were conducted, we chose comparison cohorts in an area near another nuclear plant located in the Beaver Valley-Shippingport region of southwestern Pennsylvania. This design decision required us to be conservative about estimating differences in mental health between exposed and nonexposed populations. On the other hand, this strategy increased our power to infer that any observable differences in mental health status could validly be attributed to TMI per se. Had we initially chosen comparison cohorts only at a nonnuclear facility and found significantly better mental health among its subgroups relative to TMI subjects, it would have been impossible to distinguish whether proximity to a nuclear plant per se or the increased stress of exposure to the TMI accident had produced the observed effects. Fortunately, we were able to add a second comparison group from another western Pennsylvania community that was ecologically similar to TMI but in which a fossil-fueled, rather than a nuclear power station, was located during subsequent waves of data collection in 1981 and 1982. Thus, our strengthened design would later permit us more adequately to eliminate rival hypotheses for explaining the implications of our findings.

The third key design issue pertained to the types of data that should be collected to determine whether TMI produced long-term psychiatric consequences. Most stress research has relied on symptom inventories that measure a subject's current mental health status (Dohrenwend and Dohrenwend 1981). As the Dohrenwends have shown, however, symptoms and behaviors elicited by such inventories tend to be transitory and, therefore, less informative for longitudinal assessment purposes. Furthermore, because the time of symptom onset is not recorded in the majority of these measurement instruments, their utility for determining causality is diminished. As an alternative to symptom inventories, disaster researchers have used open-ended questionnaires that encourage subjects to describe how the disaster affected them. However, the probability of retrospective distortion when using this approach is exceedingly high, particularly when legal suits are pending.

Given these precedents and problems, we decided to focus the TMI study on depression and anxiety disorders at both the clinical and subclinical levels. The clinical-level data were based on SADS-L interviews (Endicott and Spitzer 1978) and Research Diagnostic Criteria (Spitzer et al. 1978), which in 1979 were the only U.S. diagnostic instruments with established psychometric properties pertinent to nonpatient samples. The use of the SADS-L permitted us to elicit time of onset independent of the nuclear accident and thus to analyze whether this event altered the illness's natural course. Current subclinical-symptom level was also assessed so that even if the incidence of diagnosable clinical disorder were found to be low, we could determine whether symptomatology was elevated by the stress associated with TMI. The Symptom Checklist-90 subscale (SCL-90) (Derogatis 1977) was used to assess the latter level of pathology because of the wide range of symptoms measured by its nine presumably independent symptom dimensions. Since determining from our data that these nine subscales are highly intercorrelated (Greenhouse et al. 1984), we have relied on the SCL-90's overall summary measure for most of our analyses.

Having decided on the need to collect clinical data, we next considered who should be hired to conduct the interviews and how such persons should be trained. We mentioned previously that the SADS-L had been chosen for diagnostic purposes because, in 1979, it was the only instrument available with adequate reliability and validity when administered to an untreated sample. However, the SADS-L must be administered by experienced clinicians. This methodological requirement turned out to be remarkably feasible and straightforward. Although the study sites were nonurban, we were able to recruit and train qualified interviewers who had at least a master's degree (many with Ph.D.s) in a mental health field and who had five or more years of clinical experience. Moreover, these interviewers were highly dedicated employees; most continued with the field work throughout the full three and a half years of data collection.

The more difficult aspect of recruiting and training clinical interviewers stemmed from their attitudes about TMI. Just as research subjects may harbor strong opinions about the causal links between exposure to a disaster and their subsequently impaired biopsychosocial functioning, so may the interviewers share this attitude as well. (This mentality may even be shared by the project investigators!) Although the recruitment and screening process excluded individuals with obviously strong beliefs favoring or opposing nuclear energy, many professionals around the country nevertheless viewed TMI as a dangerous event with potentially serious public health consequences. Furthermore, TMI continued as a major media event, with the psychological symptoms of interest to us being repeatedly described in the newspapers and on television. The residents and interviewers in the area could not help being aware of this information. Therefore, interviewers had to be carefully trained in procedures for eliciting data pertaining to the causality of symptoms by unobtrusively probing for such sensitive material. Special quality control mechanisms were established and routinely maintained over pertinent components of the interview.

The final design issue pertained to when and how often to measure outcome. Although conclusions are more validly drawn from a greater than fewer number of data points, this decision usually is made on the practical criterion of how much funding is available. (It is not a scientific coincidence that the majority of longitudinal studies entail no more than a one year follow-up.) Another approach to choosing the time points and frequency of follow-up data collection is by reference to conceptual frameworks that predict transitional milestones in the coping process. For example, Caplan (1981) defined four specific phases intrinsic to stress responses starting with physical behavior, which enables the person to escape the noxious environment, and culminating with intrapsychic adjustment to the stress's sequelae. Cohen and Ahearn (1980) similarly suggested that responses to disaster-related stress proceed in an ordered sequence and extend over prolonged periods.

Despite the availability of such guidelines, our interviewing schedule was structured only minimally on theoretically based considerations. Instead, the timing of our initial wave of data collection in the period of December 1979 to January 1980 was primarily dictated by a very practical consideration, namely, the date when our contract with NIMH was finally approved. The first field research, thus, could not be undertaken until approximately 9 or 10 months after the accident's occurrence. The second data wave in the spring of 1980 was designed conceptually to coincide with the accident's first anniversary, a potentially stressful milestone for those high-risk individuals exposed to the accident a year earlier. The third and fourth waves of data collection, in the fall of 1981 and fall of 1982, were timed to coincide approximately with the anniversary of the initial data collection period. The timing of these later data collection tasks had an unanticipated consequence, however. Western Pennsylvania underwent massive steel industry layoffs beginning around January 1982, and thus data previously gathered at our comparison sites could potentially be used for a prospective study of unemployment's mental health effects. We emphasize this fortuitous development to show that investigators occasionally can transform nominally adverse events to their advantage.

THE MAJOR FINDINGS

Mothers of Young Children

The group clearly most affected by the 1979 accident comprised mothers with young children living near the plant. During the following year, we interviewed 312 mothers living within 10 miles of the TMI plant as well as 124 comparison area mothers. Because the Commonwealth of Pennsylvania did not permit access to vital statistics records, the samples were obtained from birth announcements in area newspapers. The TMI mothers were found through SADS-L interviews to have significantly higher incidence and prevalence rates of affective disorder during the 12 months following the accident than were the comparison site women. They were also considerably more symptomatic on the SCL-90 subscales. High symptom levels persisted at the follow-up interviews in 1981 and 1982. It is of interest that mothers in the comparison groups from Beaver Valley and those living near a fossil-fuel facility (who were included in the 1981 and 1982 interview waves) were as symptomatic as the TMI sample at the two later interview waves, possibly because of the heightened unemployment in those areas. It should be noted that the prevalence rate of clinical disorder among the TMI mothers decreased somewhat over time.

With respect to personal-risk factors for increased morbidity, both the presence of a clinical history prior to the TMI accident and being pregnant at the time of its occurrence increased the likelihood among TMI mothers of greater psychological difficulty. On the other hand, negative appraisals by the mothers of TMI, specifically, or nuclear power plants, generally, were unrelated to psychiatric status or level of symptomatology. In terms of situational factors related to outcome, mothers living within the five-mile radius of TMI, a geographic area on which considerable media attention was focused throughout the field phase of this research, were most likely to manifest high levels of symptomatology even though they were less likely to describe the TMI situation as dangerous. We found no evidence that social support from within or outside the household either moderated or mediated the stressfulness of the TMI accident, although, as expected, many social support measures, particularly those dealing with marital support, had significant direct effects on outcome status.

During the third wave of data collection in 1981, the mental health of preschool children in our study was also assessed by administering the Richman Behavior Screening Questionnaire (Richman 1974) to the mothers (Cornely and Bromet in press). As we noted above, the TMI mothers maintained their own high symptom levels over time. By 1981, however, the comparison site mothers were stressed by the impending unemployment of their husbands and became as symptomatic as the TMI mothers (Dew et al. in press). Not surprisingly, then, the mothers' reports about behavior problems in their preschool children did not differ systematically across sites. During the 1982 interview we also assessed the mental health of 150 TMI children ranging from 8 to 16 years of age and 99 comparison site children using the parent report form of the Child Behavior Checklist (Achenbach and Edelbrock 1983). Once again, no differences were found in the mental health of TMI and comparison site children (Bromet et al. 1984). Thus our findings supported earlier reports in the literature that suggested that children adjust well over time to the stresses caused by natural and technological disasters.

Nuclear Plant Workers

During the first year after the accident, 161 employees of the TMI nuclear plant and 124 employees at the Beaver Valley-Shippingport comparison facility were interviewed with the previously described instruments. The lists of workers were provided by the local unions (the largest union being the International Brotherhood of Electrical Workers, or IBEW) after extensive negotiations between them and Dr. Parkinson, one of the project investigators. Fortuitously, Dr. David Parkinson was requested during this period to provide expert medical testimony on behalf of an IBEW worker in western Pennsylvania who had been exposed to asbestos. This resulted in the quid pro quo agreement whereby the union sanctioned our research, and Dr. Parkinson provided a series of health education lectures at local and regional union meetings.

The TMI employees showed no elevations in symptomatology relative to their peers in the other nuclear plant, although their rate of diagnosable clinical disorder was higher before and after the TMI accident. This finding is probably attributable to differing personnel policies, such as transfer options, in the two nuclear facilities. In 1981 and 1982, workers at two fossil-fuel plants were also sampled, but no mental health differences were found among the three types of workers. The vast majority of workers in all of the plants did not perceive TMI to be dangerous at any of the times they were interviewed; the small minority acknowledging danger were considerably more symptomatic than the majority who viewed TMI as safe. As with the mothers, prior history of disorder and poorer social support were each found to be associated with heightened symptomatology following the accident.

Power plants are considered to be high-stress environments in which employees are required to work long hours and in which they experience extensive job tension. At each of the four interview waves, therefore, perceptions of occupational stress were obtained through the House et al. (1979) subscales that measure varied aspects of job stress and rewards. We found strong positive relationships between perceptions of occupational stress and symptoms of psychopathology. Although stress from the marital relationship and from other life events was also associated with a worker's symptom level, we found no interactive effects. Perceptions of social support also failed to moderate the effects of occupational stress.

Psychiatric Patients

The third high-risk group to be studied consisted of 151 persons who had been treated at community mental health centers serving the TMI area during the six months preceding the accident (Bromet et al. 1982b). We sought to determine whether stress associated with the nuclear accident would increase their affective symptoms relative to those manifested by a comparison cohort of 64 psychiatric patients treated in the same time period at the community mental health center serving the Beaver Valley area. Given the need to protect patient confidentiality, the staff of the participating mental health centers controlled the identification codes, and they performed the research interviews with patient groups. The patient samples were assessed only during the initial two data collection waves in 1979 and 1980 because of anticipated high attrition over the longer follow-up period.

We found that the frequency of anxiety and/or depression episodes as measured by the SADS-L was virtually identical among the TMI and Beaver Valley patient samples during the three months following the accident. Approximately 40 percent of patients in both groups reported such episodes during this period. The TMI and Beaver Valley patients also reported similar symptom levels on the SCL-90 9 months and again 12 months after the accident. When analyses of covariance were computed to control for education, age, and residential mobility, still no main effects for site were found. We therefore concluded that as a total group, psychiatric patients in the TMI area were at no greater risk for clinical episodes of anxiety and/or depression and global symptoms of psychopathology than were psychiatric patients residing in an area with a nuclear facility that had not experienced a potentially disastrous accident.

Given this general conclusion about the nonvulnerability of psychiatric patients, it remained to be considered whether some subgroups of TMI psychiatric patients adjusted more poorly than others and thereby constituted cohorts toward whom crisis intervention should be directed. By analyzing the characteristics of those TMI patients who experienced significantly more psychopathology than their local peers 9 and 13 months after the accident, we determined that clinicians should be particularly cognizant about whether their patients a) continue to perceive the situation as dangerous and b) lack a supportive social network. The presence of both factors should trigger the clinician's concern as to whether members of this subcohort sense impending doom and alienation from fellow human beings. The need for clinicians specifically to inquire about these risk variables is evidenced by data indicating that service use patterns for the high- and low-distress groups were identical in the year following the accident.

SUMMARY

The growing awareness of a disaster's potentially long-term effects has led clinicians, researchers, and public planners to consider more seriously the issues involved in longitudinal disaster research. The fact that legal liability is being ascribed for inducing emotional and somatic symptoms associated with chronic stress (Hartsough and Savitsky 1984) makes the need for well-designed studies all the more critical. As we review the dilemmas confronted in the TMI investigation, it is clear that we learned a great deal about designing epidemiologic studies of technological or natural disasters that meet both scientific and practical requirements. Because the TMI accident location was not declared a disaster area by the President and our study design was scrutinized by various professional and political review bodies (including the U.S. Office of Management and Budget), we fortunately escaped the all-too-common circumstance of having to design and initiate a study overnight. Thus, we were able to implement the refinements suggested by other investigators such as the Behavioral Effects Task Force of the President's Commission on the Accident at Three Mile Island, and we were able to draw upon earlier research regarding the effects of psychosocial stress. Our findings with regard to the immediate and long-term adjustment patterns of mothers with young children and subgroups of psychiatric patients again affirm previous conclusions about the need to identify and monitor vulnerable cohorts in the aftermath of a disaster. On the other hand, with the exceptions of prior psychiatric status and residential proximity to a disaster, our findings are less precise with regard to those personal and situational factors that affect vulnerability status. The testing of causal models of how disaster-induced stress affects physical and psychological functioning, therefore, is badly needed to elucidate the coping tasks and adjustment processes required in the face of prolonged trauma.

REFERENCES

Achenbach T, Edelbrock C: Manual for the Child Behavior Checklist. Burlington, VT, Queen City Printers, 1983

Bromet E, Dunn L: Mental health of mothers nine months after the Three Mile Island accident. The Urban and Social Change Review 14:12–15, 1981

Bromet E, Schulberg H, Dunn L: Reactions of psychiatric patients to the Three Mile Island nuclear accident. Arch Gen Psychiatry 39:725–730, 1982a.

Bromet E, Hough L, Connell M: Mental health of children near the Three Mile Island reactor. Journal of Preventive Psychiatry 2:275–301, 1984

Bromet E, Parkinson D, Schulberg H, et al: Mental health of residents near the Three Mile Island reactor: a comparative study of selected groups. Journal of Preventive Psychiatry 1:225–276, 1982b

Brown G, Harris T: Social Origins of Depression: A Study of Psychiatric Disorder in Women. New York, Free Press, 1978

Caplan G: Mastery of stress: psychosocial aspects. Am J Psychiatry 138:413–420, 1981

Cohen, R, Ahearn F: Handbook for Mental Health Care of Disaster Victims. Baltimore, Johns Hopkins University Press, 1980

Cornely P, Bromet E: Prevalence of behavior problems in three year old children living near Three Mile Island: a comparative analysis. J Child Psychol Psychiatry (in press)

Derogatis L: The SCL-90 Manual I: Scoring, Administration and Procedures for the SCL-90. Baltimore, Johns Hopkins University School of Medicine, Clinical Psychometrics Unit, 1977

Dew MA, Bromet E, Schulberg H: A comparative analysis of two community stressors' long-term mental health effects. Am J Comm Psychol (in press)

Dohrenwend BP, Dohrenwend BS, Kasl S, et al: Technical staff analysis report on behavioral effects. Unpublished paper presented to the President's Commission on the Accident at Three Mile Island, 1979

Dohrenwend BP, Dohrenwend BS, Warheit G, et al: Stress in the community: a report to the President's Commission on the Accident at Three Mile Island. Ann NY Acad Sci 365:159–174, 1981

Dohrenwend BP, Pearlin L, Clayton P, et al: Report on stress and life events, in Stress and Human Health. Edited by Elliott G, Eisdorfer C. New York, Springer, 1982

Dohrenwend BS, Dohrenwend BP (eds): Stressful Life Events and Their Contexts. New York, Prodist, 1981

Endicott J, Spitzer R: A diagnostic interview: the Schedule for Affective Disorders and Schizophrenia. Arch Gen Psychiatry 33:766–771, 1978

Fried M: Endemic stress: the psychology of resignation and the politics of scarcity. Am J Orthopsychiatry 52:4–19, 1982

Gleser G, Green B, Winget C: Prolonged Psychosocial Effects of Disaster: A Study of Buffalo Creek. New York, Academic Press, 1981

Greenhouse J, Bromet E, Dew MA: Tracking of psychological symptoms. Unpublished paper presented at the Annual Consultant Meeting of the Clinical Research Center for Affective Disorders, Western Psychiatric Institute and Clinic, Pittsburgh, PA, October 1984

Hartsough D, Savitsky J: Three Mile Island: psychology and environmental policy at a crossroads. Am Psychol 39: 1113–1122, 1984

Hocking F: Extreme environmental stress and its significance for psychopathology. Am J Psychother 24:4–26, 1970

House J, McMichael A, Wells J, et al: Occupational stress and health among factory workers. J Health Soc Behav 20:139–160, 1979

Janis I: The psychological effects of warning, in Man and Society in Disaster. Edited by Baker G, Chapman D. New York, Basic Books, 1962

Kinston W, Rosser R: Disaster: effects on mental and physical state. J Psychosom Res 18:437–456, 1974

Lazarus R, Cohen J, Folkman S, et al: Psychosocial stress and adaptation: some unresolved issues, in Selye's Guide to Stress Research, Volume I. Edited by Selye H. New York, Van Nostrand Reinhold, 1980

Lifton R: Death in Life: Survivors of Hisoshima. New York, Random House, 1967

Moss P, Plewis I: Mental distress in mothers of preschool children. Psychol Med 7:641–652, 1977

Parkinson D, Bromet E: Correlates of mental health in nuclear and coal-fired power plant workers. Scand J Work Environment Health 9:341–345, 1983

Quarantelli E, Dynes R: When disaster strikes. New Society 4:5–9, 1973

Richman N: The effects of housing on preschool children and their mothers. Dev Med Child Neurol 16:530–558, 1974

Richman N: Behavior problems in preschool children: family and social factors. Br J Psychiatry 131:523–527, 1977

Schulberg H, Dew MA, Bromet E: The TMI nuclear accident and patterns of long-term stress: implications for disaster intervention. Presented at the Federal Emergency Management Agency/National Institute of Mental Health conference, "Role-Conflict and Support for Emergency Workers," Washington, DC, December 1984

Spitzer R, Endicott J, Robins E: Research diagnostic criteria: rationale and reliability. Arch Gen Psychiatry 35:773–785, 1978

Weissman M, Myers J: Affective disorders in a U.S. urban community. Arch Gen Psychiatry 35:1304-1311, 1978

2

Impact of Disaster on Previously Assessed Mental Health

Lee N. Robins, Ph.D.
Ruth L. Fischbach, Ph.D.
Elizabeth M. Smith, Ph.D.
Linda B. Cottler, M.P.H.
Susan D. Solomon, Ph.D.
Evelyn Goldring, M.A.T.

2

Impact of Disaster on Previously Assessed Mental Health

In this chapter we report the results from one portion of a study on the health effects of environmental hazards that was carried out in Missouri during 1983 and 1984. It deals with the experiences of individuals who were interviewed as part of the Epidemiologic Catchment Area (ECA) project. The ECA project estimated the prevalence and incidence of specific psychiatric disorders in the general population. The project was carried out at five sites—New Haven, Baltimore, St. Louis, North Carolina, and Los Angeles—and included about 21,000 respondents, approximately 18,500 of whom were residents in the community and 2,500 of whom were institutionalized. Respondents participated in two in-person interviews that were separated in time by about one year. Also, an additional interview was conducted by telephone with the community sample halfway between the times of the two in-person interviews.

This research was supported by grant no. U01 MH 33883 of the Epidemiological Catchment Area Program, a series of five epidemiologic studies performed by independent research teams in collaboration with staff of the Division of Biometry and Epidemiology of the National Institute of Mental Health; by Research Scientist Award MH 00334; by U.S. Public Health Service Grant MH 14677; and by the MacArthur Foundation Risk Factor Network.

The in-person interviews assessed psychiatric disorders according to criteria in the *Diagnostic and Statistical Manual of Mental Disorders (Third Edition)* (American Psychiatric Association 1980). For the assessment interview we used the Diagnostic Interview Schedule (DIS), written for this purpose by members of the Washington University group (Robins et al. 1981), who were also responsible for the project at the St. Louis site. The DIS is a fully structured precoded interview for which symptom counts and diagnoses are made by a computer. Although the DIS was used at all sites, there were local options that allowed some diagnostic sections to be excluded. The entire DIS was used in the first interview at the St. Louis site. Between the two in-person interviews, questions that covered additional diagnoses were written. The diagnoses of posttraumatic stress disorder and generalized anxiety, which were added to the second in-person St. Louis interview, are of particular interest to the present study.

At the same time that the second wave of in-person interviews was being completed in the St. Louis site, a series of disasters occurred in the more rural areas that were being included in the survey. These disasters included remarkable floods in December, a time of year in which floods are rare. Next, within a few weeks of the floods it was announced that some roads and stables in the area, all contaminated by waste oil containing dioxin sprayed 10 years earlier, were still toxic. Officials also reported that radioactive waste in government-owned quarries had leached into the public water supply, causing some public wells to have levels of radiation that exceeded maximum acceptable standards. In addition to these disasters, a series of tornados occurred in the same general area.

The appearance of these hazards just as this survey of the mental health of the community was being completed offered a remarkable opportunity. It allowed us to return to the respondents who lived in areas affected by the disasters in order to learn whether exposure to floods or tornados or notification of long-standing exposure to dioxin and radioactive water had had an effect on their psychiatric status. We could judge this effect by comparing changes in their mental health status with changes in the mental health of a control group also previously interviewed. Respondents in the control group lived in similar areas but were thought not to have been directly exposed to the disasters.

Accordingly, we returned to the field with a new interview, the DIS/DS (DS for "Disaster Supplement"), shortly before the first anniversary of the disasters. At the same time we interviewed residents of other nearby disaster areas, including the infamous Times Beach, as well as control respondents for these groups. In this chapter, however, we will discuss only the samples previously assessed as part of the ECA project. (For an assessment of the effects of these environmental hazards on the total sample, see Chapter 3 of this monograph. Chapter 3 also provides a brief chronology of the experiences of residents in the areas that suffered the disasters and a description of the methods used in the current study.) A more complete chronology of the disasters that occurred in Eastern Missouri has been reported by Smith (1984).

Because reports of symptoms prior to the disasters had been collected independently and prospectively from the respondents who had participated in the ECA project, their reports were not subject to possible retrospective bias. It also was the case that the ECA sample came from a more conventional population in terms of marital and job stability than did the new samples and controls from Times Beach and the other exposed areas. The present report therefore offers the opportunity to witness effects of disaster in a stable rural population.

The report on the total disaster sample (Chapter 3) shows that despite efforts to choose control samples from areas with comparable geographic features and similar economic well-being, nonexposed subjects tended to have more stable marriages and, in the postdisaster year, higher incomes. Although some of these differences may have been due to the disaster itself, there is reason to suspect that risk of exposure to these disasters may itself be related to socioeconomic differentials. Lower-income individuals frequently live in areas particularly at risk of floods and tornados. Tornados, for example, typically do more damage to residents of trailer parks than to residents of brick houses; likewise, land along a riverbank that is repeatedly flooded in the spring provides inexpensive homesites. Little is known about whether persons with preexisting mental disorders have an increased liability to disaster. However, the frequent finding of high rates of mental disorder in low-income groups, a finding replicated in the St. Louis ECA data, suggests that poor mental health might be associated with an increased risk of disaster simply because it is associated with low income.

The fact that the mental health of both exposed and unexposed samples was assessed prior to the disasters allowed us to ask whether exposure to these disasters could have been predicted by the mental health status of the respondents, and to ask whether disaster affects mental health.

IDENTIFYING EXPOSED SAMPLE MEMBERS

To identify ECA sample members likely to have experienced these disasters, we sought the assistance of a variety of governmental agencies, including the Missouri Department of Natural Resources, the Environmental Protection Agency, the Missouri Division of Health, and the Centers for Disease Control. These sources identified areas that had been exposed to the four types of disaster (flood, tornado, dioxin exposure, and radioactive well water) in the counties that constituted our interviewing area. We then labeled respondents as presumed exposed cases if their residence at the time of their second in-person ECA interview was within one of the officially designated areas for floods and tornados, or if any of their recorded addresses since 1972 was in an area said to have been exposed to dioxin or radioactive water. Deciding whether a respondent's home was within the areas designated as exposed by the state agency was not simple because in rural areas homes are on RFD routes, not blocks. However, as well as we could, we located on maps the areas designated as exposed and the residences of respondents and then counted as exposed the respondents whose residences fell within the designated areas.

Out of 743 individuals interviewed in a three-county area made up of rural sections and small towns, we identified 252 ECA respondents whom we believed to have lived in areas exposed to these disasters. We selected all of those respondents at risk according to these calculations plus a control sample of 200 that was matched for general socioeconomic area. Follow-up interviews were achieved with 84 percent of those designated as at risk and with 81 percent of those designated as controls.

The number of individuals reporting personal exposure when we reinterviewed them in 1983–84 was much lower than expected on the basis of our interpretation of the information given to us by the various public agencies. Only 44 respondents reported personal exposure to one or more of the four disasters, and 8 of the exposed came from the group we had designated as control subjects. Two or 3 of these 8 claimed exposure while working on farmland or at stables at some distance from their homes.

The disaster most commonly experienced was floods. Out of the 24 respondents who reported experiencing flooding, 20 reported exposure to none of the other three hazards. The next most common disaster was exposure to dioxin. Of the 12 respondents exposed to dioxin, 9 reported no other exposure. Twelve individuals had been in a tornado, and 7 of these had experienced no other disaster. Only 4 people reported exposure to radioactive well water, and 2 of these had been exposed to none of the other disasters. Of the 6 respondents reporting multiple exposures, 4 reported exposure to two disasters and 2 claimed exposure to three disasters.

It is not clear why there were so few self-identified cases of exposure. We suspect that many of the radioactive well water users were not aware of their risk. Although news of the contaminated wells appeared in the newspapers, this hazard's newsworthiness was preempted by the excitement over the Times Beach dioxin experience. Many affected persons either may not have known that there were contaminated wells in the area, or they may not have identified these wells as their own water source. Dioxin exposure could also have been unknown, particularly among persons who had since moved from the contaminated areas. However, flood and tornados needed no newspaper stories or letters from state agencies to create notification.

Inasmuch as the dioxin had been sprayed on the roads and stable yards 10 years earlier, and the wells had been radioactive for an unknown period, perhaps for years, it was only the *recognition* of exposure to these substances that could be expected to have led

Table 1. Demographic Characteristics Before Exposure

Characteristic	Respondents	
	% exposed	% not exposed
Sex and age		
Males	41	45
<25	2	5
25–44	20	23
45–64	14	11
65+	5	5
Females	59	55
<25	14	6
25–44	18	27
45–64	14	13
65+	14	5
Socioeconomic status		
High school graduate	63	74
Income 24,000+	37	47
Less	27	27
Nongraduate	37	26
Income 24,000+	10	8
Less	27	18

Note. For sex and age characteristic: exposed, $N = 44$; not exposed, $N = 325$.
For socioeconomic status characteristic: exposed, $N = 41$; not exposed, $N = 299$.

to a change in the level of mental health measured just one year earlier. Biological effects of these substances might already have been present at the time of the initial interviews and, as a result, not detected in a design measuring change over one year. Consequently, we counted as exposed only those who identified themselves as having learned of their exposure since September 1982—the time of the official confirmation of the first of many Missouri dioxin sites and of several potentially hazardous wells. This left in the control group some who may in fact have been exposed but did not know it.

Although the number of individuals exposed was smaller than expected, they remained similar to the nonexposed group in sex, age, and socioeconomic status distributions (Table 1).

IDENTIFYING EFFECTS OF EXPOSURE

When reinterviewed, respondents were given the DIS again, that is, for the third time. Just like the previous administrations, this third DIS asked for a lifetime history of symptoms. Questions were added to ascertain whether each positive symptom in the respondent's lifetime had first been experienced since September 1982 and, if it began earlier, whether it had been experienced at all since that date. Because the dating of symptoms may have been influenced by the disaster experience, we accepted any report of symptoms in the two previous interviews as evidence that these symptoms had predated the disasters. We did this even if the respondent had reported in the postdisaster interview that the symptoms had first occurred since the disaster. However, if in the postdisaster interview a respondent reported a symptom for the first time and said it had begun before September 1982, we assumed that was correct, as there should be no bias, as a result of exposure, toward dating a symptom as earlier than the disaster.

In addition to symptom questions, the postdisaster interview also repeated a number of other measures that might be sensitive to changes in mental health. These included seeking medical or other professional care for problems with emotions, nerves, or substance abuse; self-assessment of general health status as fair or poor and limitations on activity as a result of health problems; report of recent problems in getting along with spouse, relatives, and co-workers; dropping out of the work force or breaking up a marriage; feeling a lack of emotional support from others; experiencing adverse life events and being upset by them; and indicators of malaise and distress such as boredom, loneliness, feeling unneeded or unfairly treated, being self-critical of one's level or quality of accomplishment, worrying excessively about money, feeling overwhelmed by life's problems, and losing interest in current events. Each of these topics was discussed only with respect to postdisaster experiences.

In addition to these questions, all repeated from the ECA interview, there was extensive exploration of the disaster experience and its meaning for the respondents.

The postdisaster interview lasted approximately 90 minutes. Diagnostic status before and after the disasters was calculated by computer algorithms. Significance of differences was tested by the chi-square statistic or by Fisher's exact test when any expected value was less than five.

RESULTS

Diagnoses and Their Symptoms

The disorder that one would expect to show most directly the results of exposure to disaster, considering it was designed specifically for this purpose, is posttraumatic stress disorder.

Before the disasters, posttraumatic stress disorder was very rare. Only two positive cases had been found at the predisaster interview that reviewed the entire lives of the 365 persons in the current report. At the postdisaster interview, we found only three new cases, one among those exposed to the disasters (2 percent), and two among the nonexposed (1 percent) (Table 2). Thus, these disasters appeared to have produced very few, if any, cases of posttraumatic stress disorder.

Table 2. Posttraumatic Stress and Disaster

	Exposed		Not exposed	
Diagnosis and time of occurrence	N	%	N	%
Posttraumatic stress disorder				
Predisaster	44	2.3	324	0.6
Postdisaster	44	4.6	321	0.9
New cases[a]	43	2.3	320	0.9
Three or more posttraumatic stress symptoms				
Predisaster	44	11.4	325	4.3
Postdisaster	44	22.7	325	10.2**
New cases[a]	39	18.0	311	7.7*

[a] Among persons with no disorder before disaster.
*$p < .01$.
**$p < .05$.

Perhaps of equal interest to whether full-fledged new cases of posttraumatic stress disorder occurred is whether there was a significant increase in its symptoms. Before the disasters occurred, more of those who would later be exposed reported having had three or more posttraumatic stress symptoms, although the difference was not statistically significant. When reinterviewed after the disasters, symptom frequencies had increased substantially among both the exposed and nonexposed, but now the difference between the two groups was statistically significant ($p < .01$). In part, this difference could be explained by the higher rate of symptoms in exposed individuals before they experienced the disasters. However, when we looked only at those who had had fewer than three posttraumatic stress symptoms before the disasters, the number passing the three level was significantly greater in those who had experienced the disasters. Still, it is noteworthy that most of those exposed did not meet even this modest criterion. Only 18 percent of the disaster victims who had had fewer than three symptoms before the disasters had that many afterward.

Disorders, other than posttraumatic stress, that were investigated included phobia, panic, depression, alcohol abuse, drug abuse, somatization disorder, and generalized anxiety. These were selected either because they were relatively common and, therefore, could be expected to provide sufficient cases for comparison, or because they were disorders likely to result from disaster-related stress. It was for the former reason that we included phobia, although we did not expect it to be affected by disaster because most of the phobias noted in the two ECA interviews were reported to have had their onsets in childhood. It was for the latter reason that we included panic disorder and somatization disorder, which, although rare in the ECA sample, had symptoms that might reasonably have been a response to stress. Depression, alcohol disorders, drug abuse, and generalized anxiety were all potential candidates because they were common, because they could have onsets at any age, and because they had each been reported in the literature as responses to stress. (See for example, Gleser et al 1981; Bromet and Dunn 1981; Richard 1974.)

Table 3 shows the prevalence of these disorders before and after the disasters, as well as the proportion of individuals who developed the disorders within the year following the disasters.

After the disasters, the exposed group had a notably higher proportion of affected persons than did the nonexposed group for one disorder only, phobia, and even that was not statistically significant. Furthermore, the higher rate was accounted for by the exposed group's initially high rate prior to the disasters, not by their developing more new cases. Indeed, the number of new disorders was very small in both groups.

It was possible, however, that exposure to disaster might have increased the number of cases with symptoms of these disorders even if there were too few symptoms to meet diagnostic criteria. This possibility is explored in Table 4. In this table, the number of persons reporting any symptoms of these disorders in their pre-disaster interviews is compared with the number of persons reporting symptoms after the disasters. In a few instances it should be noted that the proportions *declined* at the postdisaster interview even though it is not logically possible for there to have been fewer symptoms experienced over the lifetime a year later. However, some respondents failed to mention at the postdisaster interview

Table 3. Psychiatric Disorders and Disaster

			After disaster					
	Before disaster		Total		New cases [a]			
Disorder	% exposed ($N = 44$)	% not exposed ($N = 325$)	% exposed ($N = 44$)	% not exposed ($N = 322$)	Exposed N	%	Not exposed N	%
Depression	5	9	5	10	42	0	292	1
Alcohol	9	16	9	19	40	0	269	4
Drug	5	6	5	7	42	0	297	1
Phobia	23	10*	32	16	34	9	288	6
Somatization	0	1	0	1	44	0	319	0
Panic	2	3	5	4	43	2	308	1
Generalized anxiety	16	8	7	15	37	0	299	9

[a] Among persons without disorder before disaster.
*$p < .05$.

symptoms they had previously reported. No significant differences were found between exposed and nonexposed persons following the disasters.

The last column in Table 4 deals only with persons who had no
symptoms in the predisaster interview. Again, there was no statistically significant increase in the number of persons who had had
such symptoms as a result of exposure to disasters, although this
may have been the result primarily of the small numbers of
exposed persons previously free of depressive and somatic symptoms.

Tables 3 and 4 have shown that the disasters did not cause
many new disorders or cause persons without symptoms of a
disorder to develop them at a rate greater than would be expected
in the absence of disasters. However, there remained the possibility that disasters preserved existing disorders or caused relapses in
persons who had previously remitted. Most disorders are considered to be in remission if criteria for the disorder have been met at
some time in the respondent's life but no symptom has been
experienced in the period defined as the "present." An episodic

Table 4. Lifetime Symptoms of Particular Disorders and Disaster

	Predisaster interview		Postdisaster interview					
			Total		New cases[a]			
Symptoms of	% exposed (N = 44)	% not exposed (N = 325)	% exposed (N = 44)	% not exposed (N = 322)	Exposed		Not exposed	
					N	%	N	%
Generalized anxiety	16	9	7	13	37	3	293	11
Panic	7	4	14	8	41	10	308	6
Depression	48	44	55	54	23	39	181	21
Phobia	14	5*	11	8	38	11	302	5
Somatization	52	52	52	53	21	43	153	25
Alcohol	20	25	20	23	35	9	241	6
Drugs	7	7	5	7	41	0	299	2

[a] Among persons without disorder before disaster.
*$p < .05$.

disorder is considered to be in remission if some episode or series of episodes has ever met criteria for the disorder, but no episode, not even one that fails to meet full diagnostic criteria, has occurred within the "present."

Defining the present as the year since the disaster, we looked to see whether experiencing disaster had preserved those disorders evident in the year prior to the disaster or if it had caused a relapse of disorders that were in remission prior to the disaster; that is, disorders in which no symptom or episode was present in the prior year (Table 5).

Because the number of persons with any particular disorder prior to exposure was small, we have combined the disorders in Table 5. The frequency with which disorders present in the year prior to the disasters were preserved is shown in the top row. No effect of exposure to disaster was seen; indeed, there was more preservation of symptoms in the nonexposed, although the number with disorders present shortly before the disasters was very small. The second row shows relapses in persons with a history of disorder but with no symptom or episode in the year before the disorders. Again, no effect was seen.

We concluded, then, that exposure to these disasters neither engendered, preserved, nor caused relapse of the disorders of phobia, panic, alcohol abuse, drug abuse, somatization disorder, depression, or generalized anxiety.

Table 5. Maintenance or Relapse of Disorders Following Disaster

Symptoms [a]	Exposed			Not exposed	
	N	%		N	%
Present in year before; also present afterward	9	22		41	38
Absent in year before; reappeared	6	17		37	16

[a] Among persons meeting criteria before disaster for alcohol, phobia, generalized anxiety, panic, or depression.

Use of Mental Health Services

So far our discussion of mental health effects has been limited by the diagnostic rules of DSM-III. A more sensitive measure might be the respondents' own decisions to seek care for problems they perceived as being psychological or related to substance abuse or their doctor's perception that they had some sort of emotional problem. Consequently, we compared persons exposed with those not exposed in terms of their visits to specialty or general health services during which "you and the health professional you saw talked about any problems you had with your emotions or nerves, or any problems with drug abuse or using too much alcohol, even though this may not have been the reason for your visit." This definition was intended to be as broad as possible so that there would be no bias attendant on the willingness to use the mental health specialty sector and, also, so that problems defined as mental health problems by either the patient or the health care professional would be counted.

Table 6 shows a slightly greater use of mental health services among those exposed both in the year before and the year following the disasters, but the differences are not statistically significant for either period. More of those who had not been users in the previous year became users if they were exposed to disaster, but again, the increase was not statistically significant. Thus we again show no significant effects of disaster on mental health.

Physical Health

It is possible that there was no increase in reported psychiatric symptoms or in the number of people seeking care for emotional problems following exposure to these disasters because respondents were misinterpreting their psychiatric symptoms as physical problems. Such a misinterpretation could have been encouraged by the media's warnings that dioxin and radioactive well water might cause physical ailments.

Table 7 shows that this explanation may be correct at least in part. More of those exposed than nonexposed to disaster said that their health at present was only poor or fair (27 percent versus 17 percent, $p < .01$). However, more of those who were exposed had reported only poor or fair health even before exposure (28 percent versus 14 percent $p < .05$). This suggests that the postdisaster state might be only a continuation of predisaster differences. We found, however, that this was not the whole story. The exposed individuals who had been in excellent or good health before the disorder

Table 6. Mental Health Care Since Disaster

Health care received	Exposed		Not exposed	
	N	%	N	%
In the year before disaster	44	7	322	5
Since the disaster	44	9	322	7
Since the disaster if none in the previous year	41	10	305	5

Table 7. Health and Disaster

Health status	% exposed	% not exposed
GHS predisaster*	(N = 44)	(N = 325)
Excellent	27	41
Good	45	45
Fair	23	12
Poor	5	2
GHS postdisaster**	(N = 44)	(N = 322)
Excellent	16	39
Good	57	44
Fair	20	14
Poor	7	3
Decline from excellent or good status*	(N = 32) 34	(N = 279) 21
Limitations on activity	(N = 44) 30	(N = 322) 27
New limitations on activity postdisaster [a]	(N = 34) 24	(N = 261) 23

Note. GHS = general health status.
[a] Among persons with no limitations before disaster.
  *$p < .05$.
 **$p < .01$.

showed more decline in status than those not exposed (34 percent versus 21 percent, $p < .05$). On the other hand, no evidence was found that exposure contributed to the continuity of poor health. About half of those in poor or fair health in both groups improved to good or excellent health within a year.

Although there does appear to have been an adverse effect on those initially in good health, this global evaluation of health was taken immediately after a full discussion of the disaster experience, and so it was subject to bias. It was followed by more concrete questions, including whether illness or injuries had limited the respondent's ability to be active, whether health services had been used, and whether specific physical symptoms had been experienced and, if so, when. One would expect greater specificity to reduce the likelihood of bias. And, indeed, no significant differences between exposed and nonexposed respondents were found with respect to any of these concrete evidences for poor health. As can be seen in the lower half of Table 7, there was no significant increase in disability either in the total sample or in those who had suffered no limitation in the year before the disaster.

We also compared frequency of visits to doctors and found no significant increase (data not shown). When we asked about the onset of physical symptoms not reported in the prior interview, among those exposed to hazards there was a significantly greater appearance of only one symptom, chest pain (data not shown). However, because we inquired about 37 symptoms, we expected one to be statistically significant by chance alone. That this proba-

Table 8. Changes in Employment and Exposure to Disaster

	Exposed			Not exposed	
Employed	N	%		N	%
Before disaster	44	52		325	64
After disaster	44	48		321	67*
Change in work status					
Working to not working	23	22		207	7*
Not working to working	21	14		114	20

*$p < .05$.

bly was a chance finding is supported by the fact that there was no trend in the exposed individuals toward more new physical symptoms.

Thus, exposure seems to be related to claims of less than excellent health, but we could not find any substantiating evidence that the health of those exposed to the disasters was really affected in terms of limitations on activity, use of services, disability days, an increase in number of symptoms, or an increase in particular symptoms.

Functional Level and Morale

The most objective measures of function available were whether or not the respondents became or remained unemployed in the year following the disaster and whether their marriages broke up. Fewer of the exposed than nonexposed were working at follow-up (48 percent versus 67 percent, $p < .01$) (Table 8). In part this was simply because fewer of them were working shortly before the disasters hit (52 percent versus 64 percent). Nonetheless, as Table 8 shows, the exposed individuals' high unemployment rate following the disaster was not merely a continuation of their high unemployment rate of a year earlier. More of the exposed who had been working at the previous interview were no longer working ($p < .05$), and there was also a nonsignificant trend in

Table 9. Changes in Marital Status and Exposure to Disaster

Marital status	Exposed	Not exposed
Married before disaster		
N	44	325
%	77	75
Married after disaster		
N	44	322
%	77	73
Break-up after disaster [a]		
N	34	243
%	3	5

[a] Among persons married at the time of the disaster.

those unemployed at the previous interview toward remaining unemployed.

Marital status, in contrast, was largely unaffected by exposure to disaster (Table 9). Most respondents were married at follow-up (77 percent of the exposed and 73 percent of the nonexposed), about the same proportions as had been married the prior year. New divorces or separations in those married the year before had occurred equally among exposed (3 percent) and nonexposed (5 percent) individuals.

More subjective measures of function were covered by questions that asked about difficulties at work, with spouse, and with relatives and friends. The topics covered included enjoyment of these interactions, being upset with these persons, mutual support, and regret over being involved in the relationship. For the work situation, topics also included satisfaction with the quality of one's own work and pride in one's job.

In the month before the last predisaster interview, those who were to be exposed to disasters had had more problems at work (22 percent versus 8 percent, $p < .05$), and tended to have more problems with their spouses (14 percent versus 8 percent), and with their friends and relatives (20 percent versus 13 percent) than those who would not be exposed (Table 10). At follow-up, they still had

Table 10. Interpersonal Functioning and Exposure to Disaster

	Exposed			Not exposed	
Problems	N	%		N	%
At work (if employed)					
Before disaster	23	22		205	8*
After disaster	22	14		216	9
Recent problems if none before	14	7		174	7
Continuation if before	5	40		19	32
With friends/relatives					
Before disaster	44	20		324	13
After disaster	44	16		322	11
Recent problems if none before	35	6		280	9
With spouse (if married)					
Before disaster	35	14		248	8
After disaster	34	9		241	10
Recent problems if none before	30	7		220	8

*$p < .05$.

somewhat more difficulty than the unexposed at their jobs (14 percent versus 9 percent) and with friends and relatives (16 percent versus 11 percent), although neither was statistically significant. In any case, the exposed respondents' small excess of problems in every case was simply due to their higher initial level of problems. There was no greater development of problems where none existed before for those exposed than there was for those not exposed, nor was there significantly more continuity of preexisting problems.

In addition to interpersonal relationships, we inquired about feelings, during the prior month, of boredom, loneliness, feeling unneeded, feeling unfairly treated, not enjoying leisure time, feeling dissatisfied with one's own performance of household chores, feeling overwhelmed by problems, lacking interest in current events, and worrying about money. These variables might be considered better measures of distress than of the presence of psychiatric disorder. We counted the number of those feelings experienced "a good deal of the time" in the last month in order to create a distress score.

Before the disasters occurred, these negative feelings were already more common among those who would be exposed than among those who would not be exposed ($p < .10$, Table 11). At

Table 11.   Distress Score[a]

	Before disaster		After disaster	
Distress	% exposed (N = 44)	% not exposed (N = 325)	% exposed (N = 44)	% not exposed (N = 325)
Score				
None	18	32*	20	31
1−4 positive	75	63	68	63
5+ positive	7	5	12	6
Change				
More distressed			23	20
Less distressed			20	18
No Change			57	62

[a] Count in last month of frequently bored, lonely, not needed, unfairly treated, did not enjoy leisure, dissatisfied with own work, overwhelmed, uninterested in news events, worried about money.
*$p < .10$.

follow-up, the exposed continued to have more of these feelings, although differences were still below statistical significance. The higher postdistress scores of those exposed could be explained by continuation of their higher predisaster scores. There was no indication that exposure to disaster caused an increase in distress level. For the exposed, like the nonexposed, increases over one year were balanced by decreases, so there was little net change.

In summary, the only effects we were able to show for exposure to disaster was that it was followed by increases in posttraumatic stress symptoms (although not sufficient to warrant the diagnosis), in unemployment, in considering one's health not as good as it was previously, and, perhaps, by slightly more consultation for mental health services. We were not able to show statistically significant effects on other mental disorders or their symptoms, on ratings of social function or distress, or even on physical symptoms that might have actually been psychiatric.

Having found surprisingly few adverse mental health effects that could be attributed to disasters, we puzzled over why this might be so. One possibility we considered was that by chance the control group had suffered an excess of adverse events of other kinds, which had had as great an impact on them as the disasters had had on the exposed group. Another possibility was that the exposed group had experienced a bountiful atmosphere of support and helpfulness from the people around them in response to their disaster experience that had adequately compensated for their stress. To explore these possibilities, we had information about recent life events and the availability of support from persons in the social network.

Neither of these possibilities was shown to exist in reality. In the six months prior to their predisaster interview, those who were to be exposed to disasters did not differ significantly from those who would not be exposed in the number of adverse life events experienced. However, in the postdisaster year, exposed individuals suffered, in addition to the disasters themselves, more adverse life events (Table 12). In particular, they more often lost jobs and lost their goods through repossession ($p < .001$), and they also moved or became ill more often (however, the latter problems

Neither of these possibilities was shown to exist in reality. In the six months prior to their predisaster interview, those who were to be exposed to disasters did not differ significantly from those who would not be exposed in the number of adverse life events experienced. However, in the postdisaster year, exposed individuals suffered, in addition to the disasters themselves, more adverse life events (Table 12). In particular, they more often lost jobs and lost their goods through repossession ($p < .001$), and they also moved or became ill more often (however, the latter problems were not statistically significant). There was no event among the eight we explored that was more commonly experienced by the nonexposed respondents. Over all, statistically significantly more of the exposed suffered at least three of these adverse events in the six months prior to their postdisaster interview (30 percent versus 17 percent, $p < .01$). The particular events that accounted for this

Table 12. Life Events and Exposure to Disaster

	Before disaster		After disaster	
Life event	% exposed ($N = 44$)	% not exposed ($N = 325$)	% exposed ($N = 44$)	% not exposed ($N = 323$)
Possible correlates				
Lost job	14	7	34	13
Severely ill	5	5	23	16
Moved	9	9	21	16
Sued or goods repossessed	2	2	16	4*
Not correlated				
Car broke down	19	23	39	39
Broke up with spouse	7	2	9	8
Robbed	2	6	9	7
Arrested	2	1	2	1
Three or more adverse events	9	6	30	17**
Change				
Loss of job [a]			26	12***
Sued or goods repossessed[b]			14	3***

[a] Among those who had not lost job previously.

[b] Among those who had not been sued or had goods repossessed before disaster.

  *$p < .001$.

 **$p < .05$.

***$p < .01$.

were not statistically significant). There was no event among the eight we explored that was more commonly experienced by the nonexposed respondents. Over all, statistically significantly more of the exposed suffered at least three of these adverse events in the six months prior to their postdisaster interview (30 percent versus 17 percent, $p < .01$). The particular events that accounted for this excess may well have been the result of disasters keeping victims from work and thus leading to loss of job, which in turn led to loss of their ability to pay bills.

The greater losses suffered by those exposed did not appear to prompt correspondingly greater social support (Table 13). We asked about four types of support: a) having someone available whose advice they could rely on, b) having someone who could be trusted with potentially damaging information, c) having someone who would comfort them, and d) having someone who would stick up for them if they were involved in a disagreement. Most people, whether exposed or not, felt that they had all four types of support in their social networks both before and after the disasters, and there had been no more increase in social support during the year since the disaster for exposed persons than for unexposed persons.

In short, our evidence shows that the exposed survived not only the disasters themselves but also an excess of adverse life events

Table 13. Social Supports and Exposure to Disaster

	Before disaster		After disaster	
Support [a]	% exposed (N = 44)	% not exposed (N = 325)	% exposed (N = 44)	% not exposed (N = 322)
Level				
Full	61	69	73	69
Partial	39	29	20	30
None	0	2	7	1
Change				
None			77	64
More			9	18
Less			14	18

[a] Has access to person(s) who can give reliable advice, can be trusted with damaging information, will offer comfort, and will support unquestioningly.

that may have been consequences of the disaster. The evidence also reveals that they accomplished this without developing psychiatric disabilities beyond what might have occurred in the absence of these experiences.

CONCLUSIONS

The present study is the first, to our knowledge, to entail a before and after evaluation of mental health as related to the experience of disaster. The results contrast with those of previous studies of effects of floods, exposure to radioactivity, and exposure to chemicals (see, for example, Bromet 1980; Logue et al. 1979, 1981; Bennet 1970, Rangell 1976; Green and Gleser 1983) because we found remarkably little evidence that such experiences cause significant effects on mental health.

We suspect that the lack of agreement with some previous studies lies both in features of the study design and in the relatively mild nature of the disasters experienced. This study had available assessments of the mental health of the respondents, as well as a comparable control group, prior to the former's exposure to the disasters. This predisaster information enabled us to show that the two groups did not differ significantly before the disasters in either demographic characteristics, which might be risk factors for new symptoms and disorders, or in most types of preexisting symptoms and disorders. Studies in which measurements are available only after the disaster sometimes may compare persons exposed with nonexposed control subjects who initially had lower rates of disorder or less vulnerability to disorder. Even in our data, there was a trend in the exposed toward greater predisposition. Before the disasters, they had significantly more phobias and more interpersonal difficulties at work and less often perceived themselves as in excellent health. Although these were the only statistically significant findings, if we look at the 25 indicators of vulnerability and distress used in this study, we find that before the disasters those who would be exposed exceeded those who would not be exposed in 17, tied with them in 5, and had lower levels in only 3.

In poststudy-only designs, it is difficult to disentangle true in-creases in psychopathology from apparent increases that result from the tendency of those exposed to blame the disaster for difficulties that may actually have predated it. This study has shown that such revision of the sequence of events can be mini-mized if, rather than relying only on global assessments of health, specific symptoms and behaviors are inquired about and if efforts are made to date the onset of these specific symptoms carefully. Such specific questions set in a life-history framework reduce the halo effect that may arise from the respondent's feeling that the disaster *should* have caused adverse effects.

The fact that the current study found little evidence that these disasters caused the onset of mental disorders, caused remitted disorders to relapse, preserved symptoms of disorders, or caused new symptoms other than those specific to posttraumatic stress disorder may in part be explained by the relative mildness of the disasters encountered by this sample. None of our respondents suffered serious injury, almost all were able to return to their homes after the emergency ended, and none of their relatives died. Although the floods were much more severe than usual and occurred at an unusual time of year, many of those affected had lived for years in areas where some flooding was anticipated in the spring, and many of them had previously been through milder floods. Notification of exposure to dioxin or radioactive well water was in fact only a potential disaster, because there was incomplete and inconclusive knowledge at time of interview as to whether the serious diseases found to occur in animals following exposure would actually occur in humans. In addition, those individuals who thought they had been exposed did not know how much, if any, of these dangerous substances they had actually absorbed. In a companion chapter (Chapter 3), we find that subjects with more severe experiences showed an expectedly greater effect. Thus, this report should not be generalized to mean that either natural or technological disaster has no effect on mental health. Nor should it trivialize the experiences of these flood and tornado victims, most of whom reported considerable upset and many of whom lost important possessions, lost jobs, and suffered serious financial problems.

Another possibility that needs to be considered in explaining these largely negative findings, in addition to the relatively mild level of the disasters, is that some of the disasters' effects were shared by both the exposed respondents and our control subjects. Both groups had relatives and friends who were involved in the disasters, and the freedom of movement of both was restricted because the major roads and bridges used by both groups were impassable during the floods. (Support for this possibility is discussed in Bolin 1985.) Further, if dioxin or radioactive well water has an effect on mental health on a biological basis, rather than as a result of recognition of the risks of exposure, there could have been a substantial number of persons in our control group who had been exposed but were unaware of that fact. The much higher rates of exposure anticipated than found suggests that such hidden cases may have been common.

As a result of two findings, however, we doubt that either missed exposed cases among the controls or the disaster-related stresses they shared with the exposed group could explain these results. First, neither those believed exposed nor those believed not exposed showed an increase in psychiatric disorder during the year following the disasters, despite the stresses that their relatives and friends were exposed to and regardless of their own inconvenience during the floods. Second, despite the fact that some of the rural residents had been exposed to dioxin and radioactive well water for up to 10 years, the sample living in the counties in which the disasters occurred tended to have lower rather than higher rates of mental illness compared with the remainder of the St. Louis sample (Robins et al. 1984). Neither of these arguments is definitive because there may be countervalent factors that explain the stability and relatively low level of the rural respondents' rates of disorder. They do, however, suggest that the disaster experience was not a major contributor to the psychiatric status of exposed individuals.

Despite all these caveats, it still may seem surprising that there was no significant increase in cases of posttraumatic stress disorder (PTSD), a diagnostic category designed for such experiences. The lack of new cases may stem from the stringent criteria for this disorder contained in DSM-III. This is a disorder new to the official psychiatric nomenclature, and there had been no empirical study of it at the time it was included in DSM-III. Among the required symptoms is "numbing of responsiveness to or reduced involvement with the external world." We found few disaster victims with this symptom. Indeed, they tended to seek out relatives and friends for comfort and help. Similarly Lopez-Ibor et al. (1985) found no full-blown cases of posttraumatic stress in patients who were part of a sudden rapidly spreading and catastrophic epidemic in Spain, although most of them suffered insomnia, depression, anxiety, and irritability. The PTSD symptoms they lacked were hyperalertness, guilt about surviving, and reexperiencing the stress. (Our findings and those of others have been taken into consideration in redesigning the criteria for this disorder in the revision of DSM-III currently underway. As a result the absence of numbing will no longer be sufficient to rule out the diagnosis.)

We conclude then that disasters of the level experienced in the winter of 1982 and spring of 1983 by residents of St. Charles, Warren, and Lincoln counties, given the provision of supports available to those affected, had little impact on mental health. The more serious results appear to have been economic. There was substantial job loss and loss of property, with corresponding loss of income and assets. The impressive finding is that people can tolerate severe upset, temporary dislocation, and financial reverses without showing profound effects on mental health. Our efforts to show that their good mental health outcomes could be explained by their avoidance of other adverse life events or the rallying round of friends and supporters failed. The explanation for our findings seems to be that humans are resilient, not that their ability to overcome adverse experience depends on some compensation in another sphere for their adversity.

REFERENCES

American Psychiatric Association: Diagnostic and Statistical Manual of Mental Disorders Washington, DC, American Psychiatric Association, 1980

Bennet G: Bristol floods 1968: controlled survey of effects on health of local community disaster. Br Med J 3:454–458, 1970

Bolin R: Disaster characteristics and psychosocial impacts, in Disasters and Mental Health: Selected Contemporary Perspectives (DHHS Publication No. (ADM) 85–1421). Edited by Sowder BJ. Rockville, MD, National Institute of Mental Health, 1985

Bromet E: Three Mile Island: Mental Health Findings. Pittsburgh, PA, Western Psychiatric Institute and Clinic and the University of Pittsburgh, 1980

Bromet E, Dunn L: Mental health of mothers nine months after the Three Mile Island accident. Urban and Social Change Review 14(2): 12–15, 1981

Gleser GC, Green BL, Winget C: Prolonged Psychosocial Effects of Disaster—A Study of Buffalo Creek. New York: Academic Press, 1981

Green BL, Gleser F: Stress and long-term psychopathology in survivors of the Buffalo Creek disaster, in Origins of Psychopathology: Problems in Research and Public Policy. Edited by Ricks DF, Dohrenwend BS. Cambridge, Cambridge University Press, 1983

Logue JN, Hansen H, Struening E: Emotional and physical distress following Hurricane Agnes in Wyoming Valley of Pennsylvania. Public Health Rep 94(6):495–502, 1979

Logue JN, Hansen H, Struening E: Some indications of the long-term health effects of a natural disaster. Public Health Rep 96:67–79, 1981

Lopez-Ibor JJ, Soria J, Canas F, et al: Psychopathological aspects of the toxic oil syndrome catastrophe. Br J Psychiatry 147:352–635, 1985

Rangell L: Discussion of the Buffalo Creek disaster: the course of psychic trauma. Am J Psychiatry 133(3):313–316, 1976

Richard WC: Crisis intervention services following natural disaster: the Pennsylvania Recovery Project. Journal of Community Psychology 2(3):211–218, 1974

Robins LN, Helzer JE, Croughan JL, et al: NIMH Diagnostic Interview
    Schedule (Version 3). Rockville, MD, National Institute of Mental
    Health, 1981

Robins LN, Helzer JE, Weissman M, et al: Lifetime prevalence of specific
    psychiatric disorders in three sites. Arch Gen Psychiatry 41:107–108,
    1984

Smith EM: Chronology of disasters in eastern Missouri. Unpublished
    report prepared for the National Institute of Mental Health, Contract
    No. 83MD525181, 1984

3

Psychosocial Consequences of a Disaster

Elizabeth M. Smith, Ph.D.
Lee N. Robins, Ph.D.
Thomas R. Przybeck, Ph.D.
Evelyn Goldring, M.A.T.
Susan D. Solomon, Ph.D.

3

Psychosocial Consequences of a Disaster

Beginning in fall 1982 a remarkable set of events occurred to make the St. Louis area the focus of national attention. In October, the Environmental Defense Fund announced 14 confirmed and 41 suspected dioxin sites in Missouri. The majority of these sites were in the St. Louis area. Oil mixed with dioxin had been sprayed in these sites as long as 10 years before and was still present in levels well above those considered safe.

In December, a series of devastating floods swept through the area, causing five deaths, necessitating the evacuation of nearly 25,000 persons from their homes, and resulting in an estimated $150 million in property damages. Although the evacuation was only temporary for many of the victims, for residents of one flooded community, Times Beach, it proved to be permanent.

The community of Times Beach has subsequently become an

This research was supported by grant no. U01 MH 33883 of the Epidemiological Catchment Area Program, a series of five epidemiologic studies performed by independent research teams in collaboration with staff of the Division of Biometry and Epidemiology of the National Institute of Mental Health; by Research Scientist Award MH 00334; by U.S. Public Health Service Grant MH 14677; and by the MacArthur Foundation Risk Factor Network.

The authors would like to acknowledge the assistance of Linda B. Cottler, M.P.H., and Ruth L. Fishbach, Ph.D., in conducting this research.

internationally known environmental disaster area comparable to Love Canal and Three Mile Island. It was the first St. Louis area site tested for dioxin (in November 1982). A week later almost the entire town of Times Beach was covered with water as the Meramec River overflowed its banks.

Three weeks after the flood and two days before Christmas, as residents were returning to their homes to clean up and repair the flood damage, a second disaster occurred. The Centers for Disease Control (CDC) issued a health advisory that warned residents to stay out of the town because of high levels of dioxin found in soil samples taken by the Environmental Protection Agency (EPA) prior to the flood.

Residents were scattered over a wide area as they moved into temporary housing. They left behind most of their personal belongings, for what had not been destroyed by the flood was believed to be tainted by dioxin. Because the community had voted to take itself out of the federal flood insurance program, residents had no prospect of reimbursement for damages.

Relocation of Times Beach residents was particularly difficult. They were not well received in their new communities because their new neighbors feared contamination. There was also concern among the former residents themselves about the health effects of the dioxin.

In mid-February the state and federal governments agreed to buy out Times Beach, the first time the federal government had initiated a "buy-out" of an entire community. The buy-out moved slowly and was met with protests by residents who believed the appraisals of their property were too low and that payment was too slow in coming. One year after the disaster, the majority of the residents remained in temporary housing, and only a few had received payment for their property.

Around the same time, a third disaster struck. Some of the wells which supplied drinking water in the area were found to have unacceptable levels of radioactivity, presumably caused by seepage from a uranium plant's waste buried in the 1960s.

The arrival of spring brought more disasters. Flood waters again covered the area, and a series of tornados left a path of destruction.

Coincident with these dramatic occurrences, the areas involved suffered massive layoffs of the work force in many local plants. The unemployment rate in the area rose to a record high of 10.3 percent. A detailed description of these events is provided in *Chronology of Disasters in Eastern Missouri* (Smith 1984).

These disasters occurred just as Washington University was completing interviews for Wave 2 of the Epidemiologic Catchment Area (ECA) project, which was designed to assess the psychiatric status of the region's population (Eaton and Kessler 1985). To our knowledge this was the first time that an area affected by disaster had, by chance, also been the site of a careful evaluation of psychiatric status just before the disaster occurred.

The fact that only some areas of the research site were affected provided another unique advantage—a control group from a similar area, similarly evaluated for psychiatric disorder prior to the disasters. The report of the ECA sample appears in Chapter 2 of this monograph.

Although not included in the ECA project, the community of Times Beach was of particular interest. The severe flooding that occurred in Times Beach followed by the discovery of dioxin and the subsequent evacuation and permanent relocation of its residents provided a unique opportunity to study a double disaster (natural and technological) and the effects of long-term stress on mental and physical health. Essentially all of the residents were similarly affected. They suffered the loss of their homes, their neighborhood, and their community, and they experienced a threat to their health as a result of dioxin exposure.

In contrast to the Times Beach sample, those who were exposed only to dioxin or flooding experienced only temporary relocation. Although the homes of some flood victims were destroyed or badly damaged, they did have the option of returning to the area and repairing or rebuilding (as many chose to do). Similarly, most residents of the other dioxin sites, although faced with uncertainty regarding the hazards of dioxin exposure, could return to their homes after cleanup procedures were completed. Neither of these single disaster groups experienced the total loss of community that the Times Beach group experienced.

THEORETICAL FRAMEWORK

Disaster has been defined as a situation of massive, collective stress (Kinston and Rosser 1974). The psychological consequences of disaster are the result of the combined individual stress reactions and of reactions to change in the social milieu.

Berren et al. (1980) suggested that to understand and predict psychological reactions to disasters one must first recognize the important characteristics that differentiate disasters from one another. They pointed out that the term *victims*, in reality, describes a heterogeneous group that experiences varying consequences as a result of the types and levels of disaster exposure. They proposed a five-factor disaster typology to be used conceptually to distinguish one disaster from another. These factors include the following: type of disaster (natural versus technological), duration, degree of personal impact, potential for recurrence, and control over future impact.

Dioxin exposure, which might be characterized as a "localized environmental disaster," differs from natural disasters in several important ways. First, the threat to be faced is an ongoing condition, discovered only after a prolonged period of investigation. This characteristic clearly differentiates it from more traditional disasters such as floods or tornados where the threat appears suddenly and is immediately obvious to everyone affected by it.

Second, the scope of the problem is uncertain. A localized environmental disaster has no clear geographic boundaries, and there is usually some uncertainty as to how much of a threat it poses. Here again there is a marked contrast with an event such as a flood in which it is quite clear where the water is and what kinds of danger it might pose, although there may be secondary effects like contamination of the water supply.

Finally, exposure to dioxin is pervasive and inescapable. It is pervasive because the inhalation of vapors and contaminated dust thought to be the route of exposure touches everyone in the area, and it is inescapable because the victims become aware of it only after long-term exposure has already occurred.

These features should have important consequences for the

victims. They are faced with an entirely new kind of demand on their abilities and resources—coping with an unnatural event.

Although there is an extensive body of literature on various aspects of disaster, there has been little comparative study of reactions to natural versus technological disasters. We do not know if these two types of disasters produce different types of reactions.

This chapter focuses on two questions: 1) What are the effects of disaster on mental health? and 2) Do different types of disaster produce different levels and types of psychiatric consequences?

SUBJECTS AND METHOD

The study population was drawn from three sources. Four hundred fifty-two subjects were from Mental Health Catchment Area 27, a three-county-mixed small-town–rural area that forms the rural fringe of the St. Louis metropolitan area.

Using government designations of residential areas as exposed or not exposed, all previously interviewed ECA respondents in these three counties who were believed to have been exposed to at least one of the disasters and a random one half of those likely not to have been exposed were selected.

Because of our interest in dioxin exposure and the small number of persons exposed to dioxin in the ECA area, 100 households were selected at random from five confirmed dioxin sites in the St. Louis area. Eighty of these households were drawn from the 800 Times Beach households. An additional 20 households were selected from the approximately 200 households in the four dioxin sites where no flooding had occurred. As none of these households had been included in the ECA project, it was necessary to choose a respondent from each. Kish Tables were used to select one adult respondent from each eligible household (Kish 1965).

A comparison group of 100 cases was randomly selected from households located on a flood plain in Catchment Area 27 thought to be comparable to the dioxin-exposed sample in socioeconomic status. These households had been listed for possible inclusion in the ECA project, but random selection of neighborhoods had left them out of that survey.

Data were collected over an 8-month period beginning in November 1983, approximately 11 months after the onset of the disasters. Field work was conducted by Survey Research Associates, the same interviewers who had conducted interviews for Wave 2 of the ECA project.

A structured interview, the Diagnostic Interview Schedule/Disaster Supplement (DIS/DS; Robins and Smith 1983) was designed for use in this study. It included a modified version of the NIMH Diagnostic Interview Schedule (Robins 1983), selected questions from the ECA interview, as well as disaster-specific questions designed to ascertain the type and severity of the hazards experienced.

The modified DIS/DS permitted us to make the 12 *Diagnostic and Statistical Manual of Mental Disorders (Third Edition) (DSM-III;* American Psychiatric Association 1980) diagnoses shown in Table 1. Diagnoses with low-prevalence rates in the ECA survey (for example, schizophrenia and obsessive-compulsive disorder) were excluded.

Respondents were asked whether they had ever experienced each symptom of the diagnoses covered. Psychiatric symptoms

Table 1. *DSM-III* Disorders Included in Hazards Study

Disorder and diagnosis
Affective
Major depression, single and recurrent episodes
Dysthmia
Substance use
Tobacco use
Alcohol abuse/dependence
Drug abuse/dependence
Anxiety/Somatic
Phobias
Panic
Somatization
Generalized anxiety
Posttraumatic stress disorder
Anorexia
Personality
Antisocial personality (adult component)

Note. DSM-III = *Diagnostic and Statistical Manual of Mental Disorders (Third Edition).*

were scored as positive if they met criteria for clinical significance and were not explained entirely by physical illness or substance ingestion. For each positive symptom, onset and recency were obtained. Thus information was available as to the presence or absence of each symptom during the interval between the disaster and the interview, both during the year before the disaster and more than a year before the disaster.

In addition to information about symptoms, respondents were asked about the year since the disasters with respect to their health and disability status and changes in their health status, use of health services and psychoactive drugs, role function, social support, family history of psychiatric disorder, and changes in employment and marital status. The disaster section elicited information on exposure of respondents as well as friends and relatives, personal beliefs regarding the effects of exposure, personal and property losses experienced and the extent of recovery, use of community agencies and evaluation of their helpfulness, the relocation experience, and evidence for symptoms of posttraumatic stress in other members of the household. All respondents were asked to evaluate news coverage of the disaster, whether victims had been stigmatized and on whom they blamed the disaster(s), and whether other stressful life events had occurred in the past year.

The interviews required approximately 90 minutes and were administered in the subjects' homes. A total of 547 individuals were interviewed. The refusal rate was 8 percent for the sample. It was highest (10 percent) among those in the ECA sample who had been interviewed previously.

STATISTICAL ANALYSIS

We first classified our subjects into three groups on the basis of maximum level of exposure: direct, indirect only, and no exposure. Forty percent of the interviewed sample had personally experienced one or more disasters, 24 percent were only indirectly affected through the exposure of relatives or close friends, and 36 percent had no disaster exposure. In order to examine the differential effects of specific types of disasters, we divided the direct exposure subjects into three groups on the basis of type of exposure (see Table 2). These groups were: flood and dioxin (Times Beach) ($N = 69$), flood only ($N = 75$), and dioxin only ($N = 29$).

Because of their small number, we excluded from our analysis subjects who had experienced only layoffs or exposure to hazardous materials in the work place, or exposure only to radioactive well water, tornados, or various combinations of these disasters.

Chi square and t tests were used to test statistically significant differences between the groups. Differences at the 0.05 level of statistical confidence were considered significant.

Two-tailed tests of significance were used for predisaster comparisons between groups, and one-tailed tests were used to compare the exposure types for postdisaster measurements on the basis of the expectation that the exposed groups would have negative outcomes as a result of their exposure. Respondents with each level of exposure were compared with the other two groups. If the direct exposure group was found to differ, the type of exposure was examined to see whether the difference could be explained by a single type of exposure. Finally, level of exposure was entered into multiple regression along with other determinants of the number of psychiatric symptoms since the disaster and into logistic regression along with other predictors of a positive psychiatric diagnosis to assess its independent contribution to postdisaster psychiatric status.

Table 2. Exposure Categories

Disaster	Exposure	
	Indirect[a]	Direct[b]
Flood	85	75
Dioxin and flood	9	69
Dioxin	12	29
Other	26	21
Industrial exposure/layoff	7	21

Note. Direct = those individuals who personally experienced the disaster;
indirect = those individuals who were affected by disaster only through the exposure of relatives or close friends.
[a] $N = 139$.
[b] $N = 215$.

RESULTS

Sociodemographic Characteristics

All of the subjects in our sample were at least 20 years of age, and almost all were white. Fifty-five percent were female, and more than two thirds were married. Two thirds had at least a high

Table 3. Sociodemographic Characteristics of Sample

				Type of direct exposure		
		Exposure		% flood and dioxin	% dioxin	% flood
Characteristic	% none (N = 189)	% indirect (N = 139)	% direct (N = 173)	dioxin (N = 69)	(N = 29)	(N = 75)
Age						
20–39	40	57[b]	50[b]	43[d]	72[b]	48[d]
40–59	30	27	30	43	21	23
60+	30	16	20	14	7	29
Mean	48.8	41.7[b]	42.5 [b]	42.1[b]	36.3[b]	45.0[b]
Median	45	38	40	42	34	40
Sex						
Male	44	42	48	39	52	57
Marital status[a]						
Married	72	71	66	59	79	67
Separated/ divorced	8	11	18[b]	28[c]	10	13
Widowed	12	7	8	10	0	8
Single	8	11	8	3	10	12
Education						
<12 years	29	29	47[c]	48[c]	45	48[c]
12 years	38	33	34	37	24	36
>12 years	33	38	18	15	31	16
Mean	12.0	12.1	10.9 [c]	10.9 [c]	11.6	10.7[c]
Income						
Median	29,453	26,779	20,622[b]	18,240 [c]	23,481	21,704[b]
N	167	127	159	63	27	69

[a] Marital status was dichotomized as separated/divorced versus all other categories for significance tests.

[b] Significantly different from none.

[c] Significantly different from both none and indirect exposure.

[d] Significantly different from dioxin only.

school education, and the median income fell in the $20,000 to $30,000 range. The sociodemographic characteristics by exposure level are shown in Table 3.

Subjects in the three exposure levels were similar in terms of sex distributions. However, nonexposed subjects were significantly older than subjects in the other two groups. The youth of the direct exposure group was accounted for by those exposed to dioxin. The flood-only group was not markedly younger than the nonexposed.

Those directly exposed to disaster had less often completed high school, had lower incomes, and were more often separated or divorced than other groups. These differences were consistent across types of disaster for income and education; however, the Times Beach sample (flood and dioxin) had the lowest income and education and the highest proportion of divorced or separated individuals.

Impact of Disaster

Respondents who had been exposed to these disasters directly or indirectly were asked how upset they had been. As might be expected, direct exposure was associated with significantly higher levels of upset than was indirect exposure (Table 4). When asked to recall their feelings at the time the disaster occurred, 68 percent of the disaster victims reported that they had been very upset compared with 17 percent of those who were indirectly affected

Table 4. Impact of Disaster

	Exposure		Type of direct exposure		
Level of upset	% indirect ($N = 139$)	% direct ($N = 173$)	% flood and dioxin ($N = 69$)	% dioxin ($N = 29$)	% flood ($N = 75$)
Very	17	68[a]	91[a]	45[a]	55[a]
Somewhat	36	21	7	23	24
Not	47	18	2	32	21

[a] Significantly higher than indirect exposure.

through exposure of relatives or close friends. Each type of direct exposure contributed to the upset. In addition, the Times Beach group reported higher levels of upset than those who had experienced only dioxin or floods.

In order to determine the consequences of the different types of disasters, subjects were asked to enumerate the personal losses or property damage they had incurred as a result of the disaster experience. A list of 20 items that might have been lost was provided, including house, furniture, clothing, food, car, and heirlooms or mementos as well as less tangible items such as loss of work time, leisure time, or contact with family, friends, or neighbors.

Essentially all of the Times Beach subjects and more than 90 percent of flood-only victims reported significant damage to or loss of property and personal possessions as a result of the disasters (Table 5). Significantly fewer dioxin-only victims had sustained major damage or losses as a result of their exposure to the dioxin. Times Beach victims who suffered losses experienced a significantly greater variety of losses than those who suffered losses from only one of the disasters. They averaged nine types of loss compared with four for dioxin-only and three for flood-only victims.

Table 5. Loss and Recovery From Disaster and Type of Direct Exposure

Loss/recovery	% flood and dioxin (N = 69)	% dioxin (N = 29)	% flood (N = 75)	Total % (N = 139)
Loss or damage				
Yes	99 [a]	62	92 [a]	90
M kinds of losses (out of 20), if any	(9 [a,b])	(4)	(3)	(5)
Disaster caused household a great deal of harm	87[a,b]	31	36	55
Recovery level				
Not recovered	31[b]	24	11	23
Partial recovery	44	53	33	38
Full recovery	25	24	55	38

[a] Significantly different from dioxin only exposure.
[b] Significantly different from flood only exposure.

Those from Times Beach also experienced more disruption in their living arrangements following the disasters. They had moved an average of three times during the year after the disasters occurred, compared with twice for dioxin-only victims and once for flood-only victims.

At the time of the interview, approximately one year after the disasters had occurred, 55 percent of those who had been directly exposed believed that the disasters had caused them a great deal of harm. Almost all (87 percent) of the Times Beach group believed that the disaster experience had caused them a great deal of harm, as compared with less than one third of each of the two single-disaster groups. Flood-only victims were only slightly more likely than dioxin-only victims to report that the disaster had caused a great deal of harm.

It is interesting to note that one year after the disasters, only one third of the victims reported that they had fully recovered from the disaster experience. Flood-only victims were twice as likely to report full recovery than were those exposed to dioxin with or without accompanying flooding.

Effects on Physical Health

Although few of the victims in the sample incurred injuries as a direct result of the disasters, the stressful nature of the events might be expected to have affected various aspects of their physical health. Self-perceptions of current health status were assessed by asking respondents to rate their current general health as excellent, good, fair, or poor. Responses were dichotomized as good (excellent/good) or poor (fair/poor). Respondents were also asked to compare their current health status to what it was in September 1982, prior to the disasters.

As shown in Table 6, disaster victims were significantly more likely to report their current health as fair or poor compared with those who were indirectly exposed or unaffected by disaster. Thirty percent of those directly exposed rated their health as fair or poor compared with 18 percent of those not directly exposed, a significant difference accounted for by the Times Beach sample.

Table 6. Health Status and Change in Health Status

| | Exposure | | | Type of direct exposure | | |
Health	% none (N = 185)	% indirect (N = 139)	% direct (N = 171)	% flood and dioxin (N = 68)	% dioxin (N = 28)	% flood (N = 75)
Status						
Good/excellent	81.6	82.0	69.6	63.2	82.1	70.7
Fair/poor	18.4	18.0	30.4 [a,b]	36.8 [a,b]	17.8	29.4
Change for the worse	14.1	15.1	26.3 [a,b]	27.9 [a,b]	32.1[a]	22.7
Among those now						
fair/poor	41.3	44.0	57.7	52.0	60.0	63.6
	(N = 34)	(N = 25)	(N = 52)	(N = 25)	(N = 5)	(N = 22)

[a] Significantly greater than no exposure.
[b] Significantly greater than indirect exposure.

The poor status of the victims' health appeared plausibly attributable to their exposure. More of them reported a change for the worse in the year since the disaster than did other groups, and those in fair or poor health at interview had more often suffered a recent worsening of their health. All three groups of directly exposed subjects reported higher rates of health decline than the indirect exposure and no exposure groups.

Effects on Mental Health

We turn now to the effects of disaster on mental health. We begin by comparing the experience of psychiatric symptoms since the disaster. If symptoms are more common in victims it is plausible to think that the disaster experience caused mental symptoms. But it will not demonstrate such an effect unless we can also show that the disaster accounts for a greater *increase* in symptoms than would have been expected in that year.

A significantly higher proportion of the direct exposure group had experienced at least one psychiatric symptom in the year following exposure. And among respondents with symptoms, victims of disaster had experienced significantly more symptoms than those who were not directly exposed (Table 7). No difference

Table 7. Percent Experiencing Any Psychiatric Symptoms and Mean Number of Symptoms During Year After Disaster

| | | | | Type of direct exposure | | |
| | | Exposure | | % flood and | | |
Symptoms	% none (N = 189)	% indirect (N = 139)	% direct (N = 173)	dioxin (N = 69)	% dioxin (N = 29)	% flood (N = 75)
Percent with symptoms	71	72	87 [a,b]	90 [a,b]	83	85 [a,b]
Mean number of symptoms, if any	3.6	3.3	5.2 [a,b]	5.9 [a,b]	5.3 [a,b]	4.5 [a,b]

[a] Significantly higher than no exposure.
[b] Significantly higher than indirect exposure.

was found between the nonexposed and indirectly exposed groups in the experience of psychiatric symptoms during the year after the disasters.

Exposure to all types of disaster showed the same pattern, although the flood and dioxin group had the highest proportion with symptoms and the highest level of symptoms in the past year.

We next looked at the types of psychiatric symptoms that were experienced during the year following the disasters. The proportion of respondents reporting symptoms associated with each of nine psychiatric disorders in the postdisaster year, for each exposure level and type, is shown in Table 8.

Disaster victims showed significantly higher proportions with symptoms of six disorders. They exceeded both the indirect and unexposed groups in symptoms of depression, somatization, phobia, generalized anxiety, and posttraumatic stress disorder; and they had significantly more alcohol symptoms than those not exposed at all. Each type of disaster exposure contributed to the higher rate of these symptoms. Anorexia, drug abuse, and panic disorder showed no increase with exposure.

The indirect exposure group had higher rates of symptoms of every disorder than did the no exposure group, but none of the differences was statistically significant.

Although these results may seem to suggest a powerful effect as a result of direct exposure to disaster, they do not consider whether these are *new* symptoms or whether those experiencing disasters might have had these symptoms even before the disasters occurred. In order to assess the degree to which the disasters were responsible for producing new symptoms, we therefore determined for each disorder the proportion of respondents reporting a symptom as occurring for the first time since the disaster.

As shown in the lower half of Table 8, differences were much

Table 8. Types of Symptoms Experienced Since Disaster

Symptoms associated with	Exposure			Type of direct exposure		
	% none (N = 185)	% indirect (N = 138)	% direct (N = 172)	% Flood and dioxin (N = 68)	% dioxin (N = 29)	% flood (N = 75)
	Any symptoms since disaster					
Depression	26.5	33.3	48.3[a,b]	54.4[a,b]	58.6[a,b]	39.9[a]
Alcohol	6.0	13.0[a]	19.8[a]	17.6[a]	24.1[a]	20.0[a]
Somatization	31.9	36.2	50.0[a,b]	61.8[a,b]	51.7	38.7[c]
Anorexia	16.8	29.0[a]	24.4	26.5	20.7	24.0
Phobia	3.2	6.5	12.8[a,b]	14.7[a,b]	13.8[a]	10.7[a]
Drugs	1.6	2.9	2.9	3.0	6.9	1.3
Generalized anxiety	4.3	8.0	16.3[a,b]	17.6[a,b]	13.8	16.0[a]
Panic	0.5	1.4	1.2	2.9	6.9	1.3
Posttraumatic stress	5.4	11.6	23.2[a,b]	30.9[a,b]	24.1[a]	16.0[a]
	Onset of new symptoms since disaster					
Depression	14.1	21.7	23.3[a]	23.5	24.1	22.7
Alcohol	3.8	3.6	4.7	5.9	6.9	2.6
Somatization	7.0	6.5	11.6	11.8	27.5	5.3
Anorexia	1.6	3.6	1.7	2.9	0.0	1.3
Phobia	0.5	0.0	1.2	1.4	0.0	1.3
Drugs	0.0	0.0	0.0	0.0	0.0	0.0
Generalized anxiety	2.7	4.3	4.7	4.3	6.9	4.0
Panic	0.0	0.0	0.6	1.4	0.0	0.0
Posttraumatic stress	2.1	4.3	17.4[a,b]	26.4[a,b]	13.8[a,b]	10.7[a,b]

[a] Significantly higher than no exposure.
[b] Significantly higher than indirect exposure.
[c] Significantly lower than flood and dioxin.

less dramatic. Only two significant differences were found. More of the direct exposure group had new symptoms of depression and posttraumatic stress than did the nonexposure group. The only significant difference from the indirect exposure group was in posttraumatic stress symptoms.

New symptoms might have been a first occurrence of a disorder's symptoms or an increase in preexisting symptoms. To learn which the new depressive and posttraumatic stress symptoms were, we divided each group into those who had had *any* symptom of each disorder prior to the disasters and those who had not. For the direct exposure group, new symptoms of depression were clearly concentrated among those with preexisting symptoms of the disorder. Of the 102 directly exposed subjects who had symptoms of depression before the disaster, 31.4 percent had new symptoms in the postdisaster period, and only 14.3 percent of the 170 who had had no symptoms prior to the disaster developed depressive symptoms for the first time. In contrast, among the nonexposed and indirectly exposed groups, new symptoms occurred principally among those with no prior depressive symptoms. Indeed, these groups exceeded the direct exposure group in the frequency of a *first* depressive symptom. Thus, it would appear that the primary effect of direct experience of disasters was to exacerbate preexisting depressions rather than to initiate symptoms of the disorder in those previously symptom free.

For posttraumatic stress there was a strikingly greater increase in symptoms for those with exposure whether or not they had had prior posttraumatic stress symptoms. Their rate of new symptoms was eight times greater than the no exposure group and four times greater than the indirect exposure group, both with and without prior symptoms. Because the proportions reporting symptoms of posttraumatic stress before the disaster were similar (15 to 20 percent in each exposure group) and because flood or dioxin exposure was identified by 70 percent of the directly exposed subjects as the cause of their symptoms, it is reasonable to conclude that the disasters produced new posttraumatic stress symptoms in respondents both with and without previous experience of these symptoms.

Rates of Psychiatric Disorders Following Disaster Exposure

The pattern of distribution of positive diagnoses in the year following the disasters, as expected, followed the distribution of their symptoms. Meeting criteria for recent diagnoses of depression, alcohol, generalized anxiety, phobia, and posttraumatic stress disorder was significantly higher for the directly exposed group than for the other groups (Table 9). The only difference from the patterns found for symptoms was a lack of significant results for somatization disorder because of its rarity in all groups. (Anorexia is omitted because none of these respondents met full criteria.) Prevalences were 4 to 10 times greater in the direct exposure group than in the no exposure group for those disorders.

All three types of direct exposure, as was seen for symptom occurrence, contributed to the higher rates of disorder among the exposed. Although not all differences were statistically significant, it should be noted that all three types of disaster were associated with elevated prevalences of each disorder when compared with the no exposure and indirect exposure groups.

To learn whether exposure to disaster led to the development of new psychiatric disorders, we calculated postdisaster onset rates for each psychiatric disorder. Onset is defined as the accumulation of sufficient symptoms to first meet the criteria for a diagnosis whether or not some symptoms had existed prior to the disasters. The postdisaster incidence rate is the proportion of new cases in the year since the disaster among people who never met criteria for that diagnosis before the disaster.

There were new cases of only four disorders: depression, alcoholism, generalized anxiety, and posttraumatic stress (Table 9). There was a significantly higher incidence of posttraumatic stress disorder among the direct exposure group, but not for other disorders, although for all four disorders incidence was highest among the directly exposed.

When the excess of disorders in the directly exposed group could not be attributed to new cases, there remained two other possibilities—exposure to disaster might preserve symptoms of a preexisting disorder that would otherwise remit, or exposure to disaster might have had no effect at all, and the difference was explained by a higher rate of disorder before the disaster ever happened in the people who were to be its victims. To see which was the case, we first asked whether disaster significantly influenced the persistence of preexisting disorders. We defined a persis-

Table 9. Rates of Diagnosis Since Disaster

							Type of direct exposure					
	Exposure						Flood and dioxin		Dioxin		Flood	
	None		Indirect		Direct							
Diagnosis	%	N	%	N	%	N	%	N	%	N	%	N
					Diagnosis present since disaster							
Depression	0.5	185	0.7	138	4.7[a,b]	172	5.9[a]	68	6.9	29	2.7	75
Alcohol	1.6	185	5.1	138	12.2[a,b]	172	8.8[a]	68	10.3[a]	29	16.0[a,b]	75
Somatization	0.0	185	0.0	138	0.6	172	1.5	68	0.0	29	0.0	75
Phobia	3.2	185	6.5	138	12.8[a,b]	172	14.7[a,b]	68	13.8[a]	29	10.7[a]	75
Drugs	0.0	185	0.0	138	2.3	172	2.9	68	3.4	29	1.3	75
Generalized anxiety	4.3	185	8.0	138	16.3[a,b]	172	17.6[a,b]	68	13.8	29	16.0[a]	75
Panic	0.0	185	1.4	138	1.2	172	1.5	68	3.4	29	0.0	75
Posttraumatic stress	0.5	185	0.7	138	5.2[a,b]	172	5.9[a,b]	68	6.9[a]	29	4.0	75
					New cases since disaster (incidence)							
Depression	0.0	180	0.7	134	1.2	163	3.1	64	0.0	27	0.0	72
Alcohol	0.0	170	0.8	121	2.2	137	1.8	55	0.0	22	3.3	60
Generalized anxiety	2.9	172	4.8	124	5.6	143	5.3	54	7.4	27	4.8	62
Posttraumatic stress	0.0	183	0.0	135	3.6	169 [a,b]	4.5	67 [a,b]	6.9	29 [a,b]	1.4	73
					Persistence (diagnosis present before and after disaster)							
Depression	25.0	4	0.0	4	66.7	9	50.0	4	100.0	2	66.7	3
Alcohol	20.0	15	29.4	17	54.2	35[a]	38.5	13	42.9	7	61.7	15[a]
Phobia	50.0	12	75.0	12	71.0	31	91.7	12	66.7	6	61.5	13
Generalized anxiety	23.1	13	38.5	13	69.0	29[a]	64.3	14[a]	100.0	2	69.2	13[a]

[a] Significantly higher than no exposure.
[b] Significantly higher than indirect exposure.

tent case as one that met diagnostic criteria *before* the disasters and also exhibited some symptoms of that disorder *after* the disaster. We looked at the four disorders that were significantly more prevalent in the directly exposed but had not shown significantly more new cases: depression, alcoholism, phobia, and generalized anxiety.

As seen in the bottom portion of Table 9, the direct exposure group had significantly higher persistence rates than the no exposure group for alcohol and generalized anxiety. Thus, the significantly higher postdisaster prevalence rates of those disorders might be accounted for by the disasters' having preserved their symptoms. Recurrence of depressive episodes in those previously affected was not statistically significantly greater in the exposed, owing to small numbers, but it was substantially higher than in other groups for each type of disaster. For phobia, persistence was not significantly higher in the exposed group than in the unexposed; here, apparently, the much larger number of respondents with a diagnosis prior to the disaster accounted for the significant differences in prevalence.

If exposure to disaster does impair mental health, it is of interest to learn whether its effects are transient or persistent. To learn this, we asked whether psychiatric symptoms were still present in the month just prior to the interview. Table 10 shows that the direct exposure group had a significantly higher proportion of individuals with symptoms in the month before interview than did the unexposed group. The disaster responsible appeared to be flood, with or without dioxin exposure.

Among respondents with symptoms in the month before the interview, disaster victims had more symptoms than did those only indirectly exposed. All three types of exposure contributed to this excess.

These findings might at first suggest that, if anything, symptoms caused by disaster were more persistent than other symptoms. However, the high rate of very recent symptoms in the disaster victims could simply be the result of their having had *more* symptoms in the last year than other groups, not that they were particularly long lasting. The bottom section of Table 10 does test the hypothesis that they are persistent.

Among those who had had a symptom in the last year, those exposed to disasters were slightly less likely to have any current symptom than others, and a slightly larger proportion of the symptoms they had experienced in the last year had dissipated more than a month prior to interview. This probably means that their symptoms more often clustered immediately after the disasters and, therefore, had had more time to dissipate before the interview a year later. Thus, their higher rate of symptoms around the time of the interview was explained by the higher numbers of symptoms in the last year among the disaster victims, not by their having especially persistent symptoms.

Table 10. Psychiatric Status One Year After Disaster

| | | | | Type of direct exposure | | |
| | Exposure | | | Flood and dioxin | Dioxin | Flood |
Psychiatric status	None	Indirect	Direct			
% with any symptoms in last month	56	63	73[a]	80[a, b]	66	71[a]
N	189	139	173	69	29	75
M symptoms in last month, if any	3.3	2.4	3.7[b]	3.8[b]	3.6[b]	3.5[b]
N	105	87	127	55	19	53
% with symptoms in last year, who had any symptoms in the last month	79	88	84	88	80	84
N	134	100	150	12	24	64
% of all symptoms present in the last year that were present in the last month	72	63	59	57	54	65

[a] Significantly higher than no exposure.
[b] Significantly higher than indirect exposure.

Multivariate Analysis

We found that persons directly exposed to disasters had more psychiatric symptoms and more psychiatric disorders than those not exposed or only indirectly exposed. Their excess of psychiatric symptoms appeared to be due to a proliferation of symptoms similar to symptoms they had already experienced rather than to the development of symptoms of disorders totally new to them. Those indirectly exposed through friends and relatives did not differ from those without exposure.

Although these findings suggest a role for disaster in causing mental disorders, we had also found some initial differences in the exposed group. They were younger, more often separated or divorced, and poorer than those not exposed at all, and they had less education than either the not exposed or indirectly exposed. Given these indicators of a higher risk of psychiatric disorder, it was also likely that they had more psychiatric disorder and more symptoms even before they experienced these disasters. We have already found that they probably at least had had more phobias initially.

To better understand the role of disaster and its interaction with sociodemographic characteristics and prior psychiatric history, we performed three regression analyses. The first sought predictors of the number of new symptoms in the postdisaster year, the second sought predictors of the number of old symptoms still present in the postdisaster year, and the third sought predictors of the presence of any psychiatric diagnosis in the year after the disaster. In each analysis the predictor variables included the following: age, sex, marital status, education (dichotomized as high school diploma or less), the number of psychiatric symptoms with onset prior to the disasters, and the level of disaster exposure (1 = *none*, 2 = *indirect*, 3 = *flood or dioxin*, and 4 = *flood and dioxin*). Household income was not included as a predictor because predisaster income was not available and the significantly lower income of those directly exposed could have been due to the disaster. The results of the regression analyses are summarized in Tables 11–13.

We first performed a stepwise multiple regression to identify which variables warranted inclusion in a more complex model. We found that these variables predicted the number of new postdisaster symptoms very poorly. The only significant predictor was prior symptoms, and it accounted for only 7 percent of the variance (Table 11). The number of old symptoms appearing in the year after the disasters was well predicted, however. The best model used five variables: being unmarried, prior symptoms, greater age, graduating from high school, and exposure to disaster. Together these five variables explained 59 percent of the variance (Table 11). Number of prior symptoms, not surprisingly, accounted for the major share of the prediction (51.5 percent or 87 percent of the prediction achieved). Exposure to disaster was the weakest of these variables, adding only 0.3 percent to the variance explained by the others.

Table 11. Regression Analysis of Predictors of Symptoms in the Year Following Disaster

	New symptoms						
	df	r	ss	ΔR^2	F	$P<$	R^2
Source							
Model	1		1.97		38.87	.0001	.07
Error	493		25.05				
Total	494		27.02				
Variable							
Prior symptoms		.27		.07		.0001	

	Persistent symptoms						
	df		ss	ΔR^2	F	$p<$	R^2
Source							
Model	5		3466.37		139.09	.0001	.58
Error	489		2737.30				
Total	494		590				
Variables							
Married		−.29		.02		.0001	
Prior symptoms		.72		.39		.0001	
Age		.12		.01		.0001	
High school graduate		−.27		.01		.0001	
Exposure		.28		.003		.0451	

This first stage model was then tested for all possible two-way interactions. Four significant interactions were found: age and education, prior symptoms and education, prior symptoms and disaster exposure, and being married and disaster exposure. Adding these four interactions gave a final model with an explained variance of 63 percent.

In order to understand the nature of the interactions, regressions of the number of persistent symptoms on prior symptoms and on age were performed for the two educational levels, high school graduate and non-high school graduate, and on prior symptoms and married or not married for the four levels of exposure to disaster. Prior symptoms predicted later symptoms for both high school graduates and dropouts, but the relationship was stronger for dropouts. Among high school graduates, younger persons were more likely to have persistent symptoms, whereas among dropouts, older persons were at greater risk. Disaster increased the risk of persistent symptoms for those with both high and low levels of prior symptoms, and for the married and unmarried. However, the effect of disaster was stronger when the predisaster symptom level was high and when the individual was not married.

The very small contribution of disaster to the explanation of the persistence of symptoms in our original stepwise regression seems to have emanated from two sources. Most importantly, the impact of disaster was dwarfed by the importance of the psychiatric history prior to the disaster. The same occurred to some extent for the impact of age, education, and marital status, but disaster's role was particularly decreased because of its high correlation with predisaster level of symptoms ($r = .30$). In addition, its effects were weakened by its interaction with education. As noted in Table 1, those exposed to disaster had less education than the controls. Because education overall was positively associated with the persistence of symptoms, this association with low education tended to mask the impact of disaster. In the final model (Table 12) summing the impact of disaster alone and in interaction with education and prior symptoms, disaster was found to contribute 1.5 percent to the persistence of old symptoms, still a small contribution, but perhaps not a negligible one.

With regard to predicting the presence of any psychiatric diagnosis in the year following the disasters (Table 13), logistic regression found that three variables made a significant contribution: being male, having many symptoms prior to the disasters, and being exposed to disaster. The model explained 31 percent of the variance. No significant interactions were found.

Again, the number of earlier psychiatric symptoms was the strongest predictor of later psychiatric status, and exposure to disaster was the weakest.

Table 12. Explaining the Persistence of Preexisting Symptoms Including Two-Way Interactions

	df	r	ss	$\triangle R^2$	F	p<	R^2
Source							
Model	9		3691.69		89.94	.0001	.63
Error	485		2211.87				
Total	494		5903.66				
Variables							
Married		.29		.02		.0001	
Prior symptoms		.68		.39		.0001	
Age		.15		.01		.0001	
High school graduate		.12		.01		.0001	
Exposure		.06		.003		.0362	
Interaction							
HS × Sex		.08		.01		.0004	
HS × Age		.12		.01		.0001	
Exposure × Sex		.10		.01		.0005	
Exposure × Married		.09		.004		.0230	

Note. HS = high school.

Table 13. Stepwise Logistic Regression to Predict Presence of Any Diagnosis in Year Following Disaster

Variable	β	χ^2	p<	Partial R
Sex	−.95	12.53	.0004	−0.136
Number of symptoms with onset prior to disaster	.22	77.14	.0001	0.364
Level of exposure	.29	5.75	.0165	0.081

Note. Model χ^2: 182.00, $p < .0001$. Model R: .56. Model R^2: .31.

DISCUSSION

The results of the present investigation indicate that persons who have survived a disaster have more physical and mental health problems than those who are not exposed or who are only indirectly exposed. However, we found that the apparent impact of disaster is greatly diminished but not entirely removed by taking into account the fact that persons who experience a disaster may have been at higher risk for health problems and psychiatric symptoms even if the disaster had not occurred.

In this study disaster victims differed in several important ways from those who were not exposed. They were younger and poorer, had less education, were more often separated or divorced, and had more psychiatric symptoms prior to the disaster. Initial status and particularly prior psychiatric history overwhelmed disaster exposure in predicting outcome.

The higher rates of psychiatric symptoms and psychiatric disorders found in persons who had experienced disaster seem to be due primarily to a proliferation of symptoms similar to those they had already experienced rather than to the development of symptoms or disorders totally new to them.

There is little evidence that disasters are responsible for the development of new psychiatric disorders or symptoms. The one exception is posttraumatic stress disorder. However, even for this disorder, which was specifically designed for catastrophic events, we found surprisingly low rates of symptoms or diagnoses. Less than 25 percent of disaster victims experienced any posttraumatic stress symptom and only five percent met criteria for a diagnosis during the year after the disasters.

Although the low impact of disaster on mental health might have been due to the relatively mild nature of some of the disasters we studied, it was not the case for the residents of Times Beach. In addition to experiencing severe flooding and dioxin exposure, they were forced to relocate because of the contamination. They had lower incomes, less education, and were more likely to be divorced prior to the disasters and had the highest level of upset, the most loss, and the greatest number of moves afterward. Our results indicate that they experienced the most severe consequences in terms of physical and mental health. Nonetheless, the majority of Times Beach residents survived the experience without developing psychiatric disabilities. Less than one third had any symptom of posttraumatic stress disorder, and only six percent met criteria for a diagnosis. The incidence rates for any new psychiatric disorder ranged from two to five percent.

Our findings suggest that disaster contributes to the persistence or recurrence of previously existing disorders but is not responsible for the genesis of new psychiatric symptoms or disorders. The low rate of psychiatric morbidity in disaster victims attests to their resilience.

REFERENCES

American Psychiatric Association: Diagnostic and Statistical Manual of Mental Disorders (Third Edition). Washington, DC, American Psychiatric Association, 1980

Berren MR, Beigel A, Ghertner SA: A typology for the classification of disasters: implications and intervention. Community Ment Health J 16(2):103–111, 1980

Eaton WW, Kessler L (eds): Epidemiologic Field Methods in Psychiatry: The NIMH Epidemiologic Catchment Area Program. New York, Academic Press, 1985

Kinston W, Rosser R: Disaster: effects on mental and physical state. J Psychosom Res 18(6):437–456, 1974

Kish L: Survey Sampling. New York, Wiley, 1965

Robins LN: The development and characteristics of the NIMH Diagnostic Interview Schedule, in Epidemiologic Community Surveys. Edited by Weissman MM, Myers JM, Ross C. New Brunswick, NJ, Rutgers University Press, 1983

Robins LN, Smith EM: The Diagnostic Interview Schedule/Disaster Supplement. St. Louis, MO, Washington University School of Medicine, 1983

Smith EM: Chronology of Disasters in Eastern Missouri. Unpublished report prepared for the National Institute of Mental Health, Contract No. 83MD525181, 1984

The Mount St. Helens Stress Response Syndrome

James H. Shore, M.D.
Ellie L. Tatum, M.S.W.
William M. Vollmer, Ph.D.

4

The Mount St. Helens
Stress Response Syndrome

The Mount St. Helens volcanic disaster on May 18, 1980, took the lives of more than 50 people and created a long-term threat—the potential for future eruptions and flooding. The pyroclastic explosion of volcanic ash into the atmosphere has been studied extensively to assess the environmental impact on human health. Published public health reports have focused on immediate disaster planning, autopsy findings, emergency services, and potential pulmonary effects (Baxter et al. 1981, 1983; Buist 1982; Nania and Bruya 1982). In this chapter we will describe the stress response syndrome that resulted from the Mount St. Helens volcanic disaster and report the specific symptoms of the syndrome. Our study represents one of the first applications of a new criterion-based diagnostic field survey method to the study of human reactions to major disaster stress.

The authors wish to thank the following for their support in this research effort: the Centers for Disease Control, which provided the funding for this study (Grant CDC U35/CCU000 367-02-1); Sonia Buist, M.D., Chairperson of the Biological Effects of Volcanic Ash (BEVA) Studies Group, of which this research study was a part; Nancy Hedrick, Carol Simonton, and Sharon Siebert; the interviewers who worked on the project; and Elaine Steffen, who was very helpful in completing the final manuscript.

Our investigative opportunity became possible through a special appropriation initiated by Senator Mark Hatfield of Oregon. Funds were allocated to the Centers for Disease Control for Mount St. Helens biomedical research and were made available through competitive application. An interdisciplinary, interuniversity research consortium for the study of the biological effects of volcanic ash coordinated these studies, which included ash analysis, animal models, and human subjects for pulmonary and psychiatric investigations. An overview of the findings from all Biological Effects of Volcanic Ash projects has been published as a special monograph in the *American Journal of Public Health* (Buist and Bernstein 1986).

BEHAVIORAL DISASTER RESEARCH—A REVIEW

There are several comprehensive reviews in the literature on the psychological consequences of natural disasters. Kinston and Rosser (1974) have discussed studies that address psychiatric outcomes of disaster-related stress. Logue, Melick, and Hansen (1981) reviewed research on the epidemiology of physical and mental health effects of disasters. A recent edition of *Psychiatric Annals*, edited by Wilkinson (1985), focused on theoretical and treatment issues of the psychological consequences of different types of disasters for both children and adults. In 1984 the National Institute of Mental Health (NIMH) Center for Mental Health Studies of Emergencies published an annotated bibliography covering 20 years of disasters and mental health research.

MAJOR PSYCHIATRIC STUDIES

For historical perspective we have chosen several psychiatric studies for review. These are: 1) Wallace's (1956) description of individual and community behavior following a tornado in Worcester, Massachusetts; 2) Lifton's (1968) study of victims of Hiroshima; 3) Cobb and Lindeman's (1943) work with survivors of the fire at the Coconut Grove Nightclub in Boston; 4) Titchener and Kapp's (1976) evaluation of victims of the 1972 Buffalo Creek flood in

West Virginia; 5) Frederick's (1980) staging of the *disaster syndrome*; and 6) Horowitz's (1976) model of stress response and pathological intensification.

In 1956, Wallace published one of the first descriptions of the stages of the disaster syndrome. Wallace's conclusions were formed after careful review of a number of studies of victim response, which followed a devastating tornado that struck Worcester, Massachusetts, in 1953. "One can describe the overt behavior of the disaster syndrome as displaying three stages, corresponding roughly to the isolation, rescue, and early rehabilitation periods" (page 125). During the isolation period, Worcester tornado victims, both injured and uninjured, were dazed, apathetic, stunned, and usually ineffective in coping. The rescue period was characterized by grateful dependence. The rehabilitation period was marked by a mild euphoria, sense of altruism, and improved coping capacity. This technique of staging disaster response behaviors into broad descriptive phases has dominated the literature for the past three decades.

Using structured interviews, Lifton (1968) evaluated 33 survivors who were picked at random from the victims at Hiroshima plus an additional 42 survivors who were personally prominent or unusually articulate. In his book *Death in Life: Survivors of Hiroshima*, (1968), Lifton described from an existential perspective the internal worlds of the disaster's survivors. His description of the survivors' encounter with death, their psychic numbing, and their survivor guilt added insight to our understanding of this dreadful experience. Although he found that formal psychiatric illness was not common, psychosomatic symptoms and physical illness were prevalent and long lasting.

In the study of the Coconut Grove Nightclub fire, Cobb and Lindemann (1943) discovered that 14 of the 32 survivors had significant neuropsychiatric problems. Their description of the survivors' reactions and the common occurrence of bereavement among the victims enabled Lindemann (1944) to provide a detailed description of the phenomenology of acute grief. These concepts have been used widely to explain the psychological reaction to major disaster stress.

In 1972, a West Virginia slag dam on Buffalo Creek collapsed, creating a destructive flash flood that killed 125 people and left 500 homeless. A law firm that was retained by the survivors used psychiatric evaluation teams to assess psychiatric impairment. The evaluation consisted of psychoanalytically oriented family interviews and systematic observations of the family interactions. The findings demonstrated widespread psychiatric impairment, which persisted for at least two years after the disaster. This symptom complex, which was described as "the Buffalo Creek Syndrome" (Titchener 1976), included anxious and depressed mood, despair, survivor shame, sleep disturbance, and nightmares. The character adjustments that resulted were actually found to preserve the symptoms.

Staging of the disaster syndrome has undergone considerable amplification since Wallace's description of the victims from the Worcester tornado. C. J. Frederick, of the Disaster Assistance and Emergency Mental Health Section of NIMH, has been a major contributor to this literature. Frederick (1980) contrasted the effects of natural versus human-induced violence on victims. He described the disaster syndrome with five phases, which resemble Wallace's earlier description. The phases are as follows: initial impact, heroic, honeymoon, disillusionment, and reorganization. Each phase is associated with a variety of psychological symptoms. Victims of human-induced violence tend to feel guilt over their inability to prevent their victimization, whereas victims of major disasters do not. Like Beigel and Berren (1985), Frederick emphasized the importance of the type of violence or disaster and the fabric of the community in determining the disaster response.

In his long-standing studies of stress response syndromes, Horowitz (1976) contributed to our understanding of normal and abnormal psychological responses to disasters and personal traumatic events. He stressed the significance of disruptive symptoms that persist long after the actual stress, even in conditions of relative safety. At later times fears may return, for the threat is recorded in memory and the human mind may experience the threat as renewed and prepare for possible repetition. Horowitz pointed out that both normal and abnormal responses to disaster involve both logical and irrational beliefs about the meaning of the disaster. This reaction may include efforts to use the disaster to attempt a solution of some other, and potentially unrelated, life issue. Horowitz described five phases that occur after a stressful event: outcry, denial, intrusiveness, working through, and completion. Like the symptomatology of grief after the death of a loved one, he concluded that resolution of this process seldom is completed in less than one to two years.

Another area of research that has contributed to our understanding of the psychological response to severe trauma is the recent work done with military veterans of the Vietnam war. These findings have aided mental health clinicians in defining the symptoms of posttraumatic stress response and have emphasized the potential for delayed onset and prolonged duration (Figley 1979).

THE NEW CRITERION-BASED DIAGNOSTIC METHOD

Over the past decade, the psychiatric research community has been working actively to improve the validity and reliability of psychiatric diagnosis. These efforts were initiated with the development and testing of Research Diagnostic Criteria and resulted in a national effort to revise the psychiatric diagnostic system on the basis of specific behavioral and symptomatic criteria for each disorder. The new diagnostic system was officially adopted by the American Psychiatric Association (1980) in the third edition of the *Diagnostic and Statistical Manual of Mental Disorders (DSM-III)*. At the same time, through support from NIMH, selected universities were developing and field testing a structured interview patterned after *DSM-III* and designed for administration by trained paraprofessionals. This new method, entitled the Diagnostic Interview Schedule (DIS) (Robins et al. 1981), allowed broad application of criterion-based diagnostic assessment for the study of psychiatric epidemiology. DIS findings have recently been reported from three communitywide studies as part of the national Epidemiology Catchment Area project (Robins et al. 1984). In the development of our research methodology for the Mount St. Helens disaster, we incorporated the DIS. This was one of the first applications of this new technique to a disaster community.

The extensive investigation that led to the development of *DSM-III* and the DIS focused on both the validity and reliability of operational definitions for major psychiatric disorders and emphasized diagnostic accuracy as the major goal. The DIS is composed of a series of question subgroups that review specific symptoms of various psychiatric disorders, including lifetime prevalence, age at onset, severity, and duration. Probe questions for each symptom provide a differential diagnostic assessment to distinguish major psychiatric disorders from substance abuse and medical illness. For example, to exhibit the required depressive symptoms, a respondent also must tell a doctor or other health professional of the problem, take medication for the depression more than once, or suffer significant symptom interference in daily activities. Bereavement associated with the death of a close friend or relative is excluded, as are symptoms associated with a significant physical illness or substance abuse. For the Mount St. Helens study we included 14 psychiatric disorders available from the DIS in our research questionnaire (Table 1).

Table 1. Psychiatric Disorders Included in Mount St. Helens Study

DIS/DSM-III disorders	
Substance use disorders	Anxiety/somatoform disorders
Alcohol abuse/dependence	Phobia
Drug abuse/dependence	Panic
Schizophrenic/schizophreniform disorders	Obsessive-compulsive
Schizophrenia	Somatization
Schizophreniform disorder	Generalized anxiety
Affective disorders	Posttraumatic stress
Manic episode	Personality disorder
Major depression	Antisocial personality
Dysthymia	

Note. DSM-III = Diagnostic and Statistical Manual of Mental Disorders (Third Edition).

RESEARCH METHODOLOGY

Our study included two rural Northwest logging communities.
Castle Rock, Washington, and the adjoining Toutle River Valley
were severely affected by the Mount St. Helens eruption and
flood. This area served as our exposed community. Estacada, Oregon, and the surrounding Eagle Creek community were chosen as
a comparable control community. The sampling procedure included several steps. First, residence lists for both communities
were compiled from a variety of sources. For the exposed community we also had access to a property damage survey conducted by
the county tax assessor following the May 1980 eruption. To
maximize the number of disaster victims in the study, we stratified the sample from our exposed community to include all property damaged households. A systematic random sample was taken
of the remaining households. For the control community the
sample consisted of a systematic random sample of all households.
A single respondent was selected from each household using a
sampling scheme designed to provide an age-sex distribution that
would approximate that of the total population (Bryant 1978). All
respondents were required to be between the ages of 18 and 79
years, Caucasian, and continuously residing in the study area since
May 18, 1980. Only single family or noninstitutional small group
residences were included.

After our initial interviews were completed, we identified all
individuals who reported either significant residential damage, a
total dollar loss of at least $5,000, or the death of a family member
or other relative as a result of the Mount St. Helens disaster. To
further increase the disaster sample, we then attempted to interview a member of the opposite sex in all such households having
at least two eligible adults. This resulted in an additional 60 subjects, giving us a total sample size of 1,025. We divided the subjects
into three groups—high exposure, low exposure, and control—on
the basis of information obtained from their questionnaires. Specifically, the 138 subjects who suffered at least $5,000 in Mount St.
Helens-related property loss or a death to a family member or close

relative were defined as *high exposure*. The remaining 410 subjects in the exposed community were classified as *low exposure*, and the 477 Oregon subjects constituted the *control* group. Thus, the classification of subjects from the disaster community into high- or low-exposure groups was based on specific objective criteria. We were able to externally validate these criteria through tax assessor records or double sample confirmation for approximately 80 percent of the subjects.

Initial contact with potential households was guided by a protocol that required multiple contact attempts both by telephone and in the field. Overall, 81.4 percent of all households selected for screening were contacted. The contact rates for the Oregon and Washington samples were comparable, with the exception of the property damage group, where contact was more efficient (95.3 percent). The greater efficiency of contact among property damage households reflects both the composition of this group and the different manner in which the sampling list for this group was derived. Among the eligible individuals who were contacted, compliance rates were virtually identical (77 to 78 percent) among all three sampling groups. Comparison with available census data indicated that our samples underrepresented younger, single, and lower socioeconomic status individuals to a similar degree for both communities.

The field interview research instrument was developed to address multiple variables in the study of psychiatric disorder and disaster stress. The variables included in individual components of the research questionnaire were past and present mental health status, physical health history, sociodemographic and occupational status, support networks, the perception of threat and of the disaster impact, sense of psychological well-being, present state symptomatology at the time of the field interview, and use of recovery assistance. Past and present mental health status were measured using the DIS. Eighteen field interviewers underwent an intensive two-week training session and successfully demonstrated their mastery of the interview protocol, especially the DIS. Interrater reliability for the DIS case rating was demonstrated with a kappa of .93. All interviews were conducted between the months of June and November 1983, three to four years after the major eruption.

The onset and prevalence rates reported for our two Washington groups represent simple averages from among the low- and high-exposure subjects. More sophisticated estimation procedures using stratification weights led to essentially the same results. Statistical methods for comparing onset rates included both logistic regression and a chi-square test for trend in proportions (Fleiss 1981, pages 147–149). Diagnostic information from the DIS data was generated using a computer program supplied by Washington University in St. Louis.

RESULTS

Three of the 14 DIS disorders had a significant increase of post-disaster prevalence when compared with the control community. These *Mount St. Helens (MSH) disorders* included single-episode depression, generalized anxiety disorder (GAD), and Mount St. Helens posttraumatic stress disorder (MSH-PTSD). The progressive dose-response relationship, comparing control to low- to high-exposure groups, has been reported in detail elsewhere (Shore et al. 1986a, 1986b). Figure 1 presents the posteruption onsets of the MSH disorders by level of disaster exposure, demonstrating the significant dose-response effect of the disaster stress. Overall rates for both sexes increased from 5.7 percent to 21.2 percent when comparing control to low-exposure to high-exposure subjects. For high-exposure females the rate was double that for males (28.3 percent versus 13.2 percent). Differences between exposure groups and between sexes were statistically significant on the basis of logistic regression analysis (sexual differences: $\chi^2 = 7.3$, $df = 1$, $p < .01$; exposure differences: $\chi^2 = 21.1$, $df = 2$, $p < .005$).

Figure 2 reports the annual incidence of MSH disorders following the May 1980 volcanic eruption. In the first year after the eruption there was a highly statistically significant difference, $\chi^2 = 53.4$, $df = 1$, $p < .005$, in incidence from control to low-exposure to high-exposure groups on the basis of the chi-square

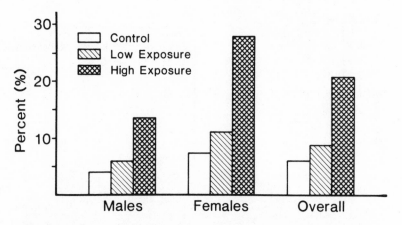

Figure 1. Onset of psychiatric disorders after eruption of Mount St. Helens. Results are based on subjects who had no prior history of the particular disorder.

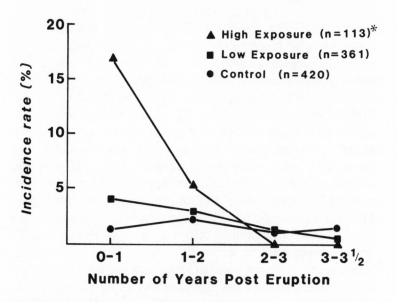

*Number of "at-risk" subjects immediately post disaster excludes subjects with prior onsets

Figure 2. Incidence of disorders following the May 1980 eruptions of Mount St. Helens.

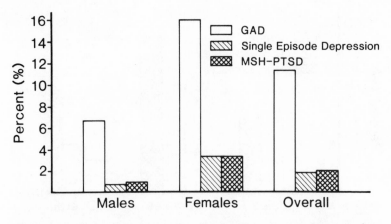

Figure 3. Type of psychiatric disorders found in community exposed to Mount St. Helens eruption. Results are based on subjects who had no prior history of the particular disorder they experienced.

test for trend. The onset of MSH disorders still appeared to be operating in the high-exposure group in the second year after the eruption but with a dramatic decline. The differences for this second year, however, were not significant.

Figure 3 shows the diagnostic breakdown for the MSH disorders in the exposed community. Generalized anxiety disorder occurred among 10.9 percent of all exposed subjects overall and among 15.5 percent of women and 6.8 percent of men. Rates for GAD were significantly greater than for other disorders among men and women on the basis of McNemar's test ($z = 3.53$, $p < .001$, for men and, $z = 4.08$, $p < .001$, for women) (Fleiss 1981, pages 113–119). Rates for both single-episode depression and MSH-PTSD were 3.3 percent for women compared with 0.4 percent and 0.7 percent, respectively, for males.

Because we were interested in identifying the complete pattern of stress response disorders related to Mount St. Helens, we included both new onsets (postdisaster MSH disorders) and the recurrence of symptoms of MSH disorders that had first occurred prior to the disaster. This combined both new onsets and recurrences to give a complete picture of symptomatic disorders that may have been related to, but not necessarily caused by, this disaster. Fifty-four subjects who had no history of a predisaster disorder experienced a MSH disorder after the disaster stress. Ninety-nine subjects, or an additional 45, experienced disaster stress symptoms if both prior and postdisaster onset of MSH disorders are included. If postdisaster symptoms of recurrent depression are also included, there are seven additional cases.

Figure 4 presents the pattern of overlap for the MSH disorders. For purposes of this figure, subjects are counted as positive for a disorder if they had either a new onset or a recurrence of symptoms for the disorder following the May 1980 eruption. Of 99 subjects with either an onset or recurrence for one of the MSH disorders, 87 experienced a single disorder and 12 experienced two or more of the MSH disorders. For single-episode depression, 5 occurred alone with 7 overlapping diagnoses. For MSH-PTSD, only 2 of 11 occurred alone. Of the overlapping diagnoses, all 12 involved GAD. Four subjects experienced all three MSH disorders. Using the chi-square test for independence and combining the overlap categories into one group, the diagnostic disorders were

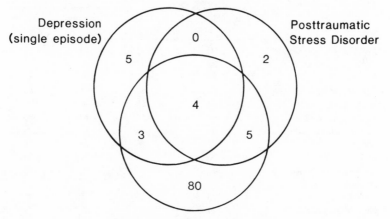

Figure 4. Type of psychiatric disorders found in community exposed to Mount St. Helens eruption. Among 548 exposed subjects, 99 experienced a psychiatric disorder either with onset after the eruption or with onset prior to the eruption but with symptoms appearing after the eruption.

interrelated at a statistically significant level ($\chi^2 = 24.8$, $df = 1$, $p < .001$).

Table 2 summarizes the symptom profile for exposed subjects with posteruption onsets or recurrences of MSH disorders. In this table, all post-MSH symptoms are counted whether or not they were associated with an overlapping diagnosis. Thus, a subject with a posteruption onset of depression may have symptoms of PTSD without having had a PTSD diagnosis. Only MSH-related PTSD symptoms are counted, however. The 16 symptoms are rank ordered by frequency of overall occurrence and are also reported for the three individual disorders. Six of the 16 symptom groups occurred with a frequency of 50 percent or greater for all three disorders. For PTSD some symptoms occurred in 100 percent of cases because they were required for a diagnosis. Avoidant behavior was the least common symptom. In comparing symp-

Table 2. Symptom Profile for Exposed Subjects With Posteruption Onsets or Recurrence of MSH Disorders

	Disorder			
Symptoms %	Any MSH disorder (N = 99)	GAD (N = 92)	Depression (N = 12)	PTSD (N = 11)
Apprehensive expectation	90	97	58	82
Vigilance/scanning	90	97	58	82
Motor tension	89	96	58	82
Autonomic hyperactivity	77	83	58	82
Insomnia	61	58	100	100
Thoughts of death	52	51	58	64
Trouble concentrating	44	42	83	100
Fatigue	37	36	67	64
Loss of appetite	36	36	42	64
Hyperalertness/startle	29	28	58	100
Psychomotor agitaton or retardation	23	25	50	45
Guilt/worthlessness	21	20	25	27
Intrusive thoughts	19	18	42	100
Numbing of responsiveness	18	17	42	100
Loss of sex drive	17	17	25	9
Avoidance behavior	9	9	25	36

Note. MSH = Mount St. Helens. GAD = generalized anxiety disorder. PTSD = posttraumatic stress disorder.

toms of the three MSH disorders there was little variation in rank order of symptoms, with or without the addition of recurrent symptoms from predisaster disorders.

DISCUSSION

This unique research opportunity to investigate the psychiatric reactions to the Mount St. Helens disaster provided data to compare the relationship of the stress-related disorders with their individual and overlapping symptomatology. In another publication (Shore et al. 1986b) of these research findings, we have documented a progressive dose-response pattern related to the level of exposure stress. The significant MSH disorders were generalized anxiety, single-episode depression, and posttraumatic stress disorder. Exposed women demonstrated elevated onset levels for all three disorders whereas men only evidenced elevated levels of GAD. Nevertheless, for both sexes the data showed a significant, stepwise increase in onset rates from control to low- to high-exposure groups. For each exposure category the onset rates observed among women were approximately twice as high as those for men. When we stratified our analysis by age, employment status, physical health history, and a number of other variables, the dose-response pattern remained consistent among all sub-groups. In addition, we tested to see if the disaster response was different for individuals experiencing bereavement versus other forms of loss. Even when we excluded subjects who reported a MSH-related death from our analysis, we still found a highly significant dose-related onset pattern for the MSH disorders in the first posteruption year.

The annual incidence of MSH disorders was significantly higher in the first year posteruption. All of the disaster-related onsets occurred within the first two years following the disaster. For individuals who experienced a new onset of one of the MSH disorders following the eruption, there was a tendency for duration of symptoms to be greater among the high-exposure subjects. Both GAD and depression tended to resolve within one to two years, whereas MSH-PTSD frequently persisted for a longer period of time. These findings are compatible with other descriptions of the persistence of psychiatric symptomatology and have been summarized by Kinston and Rosser (1974) who noted that

> the incidence of illness reaches a maximum shortly after the disaster and is compounded of caused illness, precipitated illness and illness which would have occurred at that time anyway. The incidence then falls slowly to below normal for the population, reflecting the premature occurrence of precipitated illness, and eventually returns to normal. The prevalence will of course persist above normal reflecting the existence of long-term complications. (page 451)

In a previous report (Shore et al. 1986a) we demonstrated that the relative risks associated with low exposure were highest among suspected high-risk subgroups. In the high-exposure group rates were elevated for all risk subgroups. This suggested the possibility that in the high-exposure group the disaster impact was so intense that it saturated the at risk populations. The intense stress may have overridden influences that contributed to a high-risk status at a lower exposure level. A second observation supported this saturation phenomena. The high-exposure group experienced a lower onset of new disorders in the third and fourth years posteruption compared with the control group (Figure 2).

This chapter broadens our analysis of stress response to include both the MSH disorders that occurred for the first time posteruption and the same disorders that had an onset prior to the eruption but a recurrence of symptomatology posteruption. The second definition of a stress response syndrome certainly may define a second population at risk. These individuals experienced significant impairment from their recurrent symptomatology that was undoubtedly exacerbated by this particular disaster stress. In considering the total population of victims who suffered from the disaster stress syndrome, it seems appropriate to consider carefully those with recurrent symptomatology even though their disorder was not caused by the Mount St. Helens disaster.

We found a significant degree of co-occurrence among the three MSH disorders. By either definition the proportion of overlapping diagnoses were virtually identical (13 percent to 12 percent). In evaluating the co-occurrence of symptoms using the DIS, Boyd et al. (1984) found that if two disorders were related to each other according to *DSM-III* exclusion criteria, then the presence of a dominant disorder greatly increased the odds of having the excluded disorder. They also found that disorders that were related to one another by *DSM-III* criteria were associated more strongly than disorders that *DSM-III* defined as unrelated. In general there was a tendency toward co-occurrence so that the presence of any disorder increased the odds of having almost any other disorder. We have demonstrated that patients with our most prevalent MSH disorder, GAD, had a significantly greater probability of experiencing symptoms of another MSH disorder, depression or MSH-PTSD. Certainly the broad and nonspecific cluster of symptoms required to diagnose GAD strongly influences this outcome. Sierles et al. (1983) studied concurrent psychiatric illness among Vietnam veterans with posttraumatic stress disorder. They reported coexisting syndromes to include alcoholism, drug dependence, antisocial personality disorder, somatization disorder, endogenous depression, and organic mental disorder. We did not find the associated increase of substance abuse or antisocial personality disorders among the MSH victims. Our findings indicate that the MSH stress response syndrome can be classified as a single occurrence or combination of only three disorders that have extensive overlap of symptomatology.

The six most common symptoms for exposed subjects with posteruption onset or recurrence of Mount St. Helens disorders are apprehensive expectation, vigilance and scanning, motor tension, autonomic hyperactivity, insomnia, and thoughts of death. These symptoms have frequently been mentioned in previously published reports describing the disaster syndrome. However, the particular nature of the MSH stress response syndrome may have a unique pattern that is different from the effects of other types of disasters. Frederick (1980) and others have written extensively about the specific effects of natural versus human-induced violence on victims. The low occurrence of guilt (21 percent) in the MSH disorders would distinguish this from other major stress experiences, such as victimization by terrorists. The low occurrence of intrusive thoughts, numbing of responsiveness, and avoidant behaviors is in clear contrast to the experience of concentration camp survivors and of children who have been victims of kidnapping.

The pattern of symptoms that we observed following the Mount St. Helens disaster is compatible with the staging models described by Wallace (1956) and Frederick (1980). Our findings add an additional dimension in outlining the specific symptoms, their duration, and the overlapping relationship of the psychiatric disorders. In addition, Horowitz's dynamic perspective and emphasis on the symbolic significance of the disruptive symptoms and their tendency to persist or recur after the actual stressor is an important consideration in treating disaster victims. The group of victims who were at highest risk for persistence and intrusion of the disruptive symptoms would be those who were classified as MSH-PTSD. The three MSH disorders demonstrate increasing severity, from GAD to depression to MSH-PTSD.

A recent study of symptom patterns among Vietnam veterans suggests that our current *DSM-III* criteria for PTSD may underestimate the prevalence of stress-induced impairment. Laufer et al. (1985) tested the relationship between traumatic stress and PTSD. They compared the *DSM-III* approach of aggregating symptoms with an approach that differentiated symptoms into subtypes of denial and reexperiencing. Their findings indicated that distinguishing responses of denial and reexperiencing was more useful for understanding PTSD and its origins. Furthermore, they suggested that the current PTSD model may underestimate its prevalence. Laufer's research relates to our findings of the MSH disorders and their prevalence. MSH-PTSD was only one of three significant MSH disorders and accounted for only 11 of the 99 cases.

In summary, the pattern of the Mount St. Helens disorders and their specific and overlapping symptomatology provide a detailed description of a stress response syndrome following a major natural disaster. These stress-induced disorders are described in terms of a dose-response relationship, risk patterns, severity of the individual disorder, duration of the symptomatology, and co-occurrence of the disorders and their symptoms.

REFERENCES

American Psychiatric Association: Diagnostic and Statistical Manual of Mental Disorders (Third Edition). Washington, DC, American Psychiatric Association, 1980

Baxter PJ, Ing R, Falk H, et al: Mount St. Helens eruptions, May 18 to June 12, 1980: an overview of the acute health impact. JAMA 246:2585–2589, 1981

Baxter PJ, Ing R, Falk H, et al: Mount St. Helens eruptions: the acute respiratory effects of volcanic ash in a North American community. Arch Environ Health 38:138–143, 1983

Beigel A, Berren MR: Human-induced disasters. Psychiatric Annals 15:143–150, 1985

Boyd JH, Burke JD, Gruenberg E, et al: Exclusion criteria of DSM-III. Arch Gen Psychiatry 41:983–989, 1984

Bryant BE: Respondent selection in a time of changing household composition, in Readings in Survey Research. Edited by Ferber R. Chicago, American Marketing Association, 1978

Buist AS: Are volcanoes hazardous to your health? West J Med 237:294–301, 1982

Buist AS, Bernstein R (eds): Health Effects of Volcanoes: An Approach to Evaluating the Health Effects of an Environmental Hazard. Am J Public Health 76:1–90, 1986

Cobb S, Lindemann E: Neuropsychiatric observations during the Coconut Grove fire. Ann Surg 117:814–824, 1943

Disaster at Buffalo Creek (Special Section). Am J Psychiatry 133:295–315, 1976

Figley CR (ed): Stress Disorders Among Vietnam Veterans: Theory, Research, and Treatment. New York, Brunner-Mazel, 1979

Fleiss JL: Statistical Methods for Rates and Proportions, 2nd ed. New York, Wiley, 1981

Frederick CJ: Effects of Natural vs. Human-Induced Violence Upon Victims. Evaluation and Change (Special Issue): 71–75, 1980

Horowitz M: Stress Response Syndromes. New York, Jason Aronson, 1976

Kinston W, Rosser R: Disaster: effects on mental and physical state. J Psychosom Res 18:437–456, 1974

Laufer RS, Brett E, Gallops MS: Symptom patterns associated with post-traumatic stress disorder among Vietnam veterans exposed to war trauma. Am J Psychiatry 142:1304–1311, 1985

Lifton RJ: Death in Life—The Survivors of Hiroshima. London, Weidenfeld and Nicholson, 1968

Lindemann E: Symptomatology and management of acute grief. Am J Psychiatry 101:141–148, 1944

Logue JN, Melick ME, Hansen H: Research issues and directions in the epidemiology of health effects of disasters. Epidemiol Rev 3:140–162, 1981

Nania J, Bruya TE: In the wake of Mount St. Helens. Ann Emerg Med 11:184–191, 1982

National Institute of Mental Health: Disasters and Mental Health: An Annotated Bibliography (DHHS Pub No. ADM 84-1311). Rockville, MD, National Institute of Mental Health, 1984

Robins LN, Helzer JE, Crough J, et al: National Institute of Mental Health Diagnostic Interview Schedule. Arch Gen Psychiatry 38:318–389, 1981

Robins LN, Helzer JE, Weissman MM, et al: Lifetime prevalence of specific psychiatric disorders in three sites. Arch Gen Psychiatry 41:949–958, 1984

Shore JH, Tatum EL, Vollmer WM: Evaluation of mental health effects of disaster. Am J Public Health 76:76-83, 1986a

Shore JH, Tatum EL, Vollmer WM: Psychiatric reactions to disaster: the Mt. St. Helens experience. Am J Psychiatry 143:590-595, 1986b

Sierles FS, Chen J, McFarland RE, et al: Posttraumatic stress disorder and concurrent psychiatric illness: a preliminary report. Am J Psychiatry 140:1177–1179, 1983

Titchener JL, Kapp FT: Family and character change at Buffalo Creek. Am J Psychiatry 133:295–316, 1976

Wallace AFC: Human behavior in extreme situations: a study of the literature and suggestions for further research, in Disaster Study No. 1 (Publication No. 390). Washington, DC, National Research Council Committee on Disaster Studies, National Academy of Sciences, 1956

Wilkinson CB (ed): Psychiatric Annals 15:3, 1985

5

Relationship of Perception and Mediating Variables to the Psychiatric Consequences of Disaster

Ellie L. Tatum, M.S.W.
William M. Vollmer, Ph.D.
James H. Shore, M.D.

5

Relationship of Perception and Mediating Variables to the Psychiatric Consequences of Disaster

The conceptual model that was developed for the study of the mental health consequences of the Mount St. Helens volcanic disaster (Shore et al. 1986a) was based on an interactional model of stress response. Perception of threat is identified as an important variable linking the circumstances of a disaster situation with the short- and long-term psychological responses. Perceived threat was outlined by Kates (1977) as an important aspect that determines individuals' reactions to disasters. In presenting a model of natural hazards in human ecology he pointed out, "Variation in the perception of a specific natural hazard . . . can be accounted for by a combination of: the way in which characteristics of the natural event are perceived, the nature of personal encounters with the hazard, and factors of individual personality" (page 441). The Mount St. Helens experience presented a unique opportunity to examine these interactions as they pertain to the victims of one of

The authors wish to thank the following for their support in this research effort: the Centers for Disease Control, which provided the funding for this study (Grant CDC U35/CCU000 367-02-1); Sonia Buist, M.D., Chairperson of the Biological Effects of Volcanic Ash (BEVA) Studies Group, of which this research study was a part; Nancy Hedrick, Carol Simonton, and Sharon Siebert; and the interviewers who worked on the project, which was conducted at the Oregon Health Sciences University.

the most disastrous volcanic events in United States history.

In this chapter we explore how the perceptions of victims of the Mount St. Helens disaster relate to objective measures of threat and psychological trauma. In Chapter 4 we described the psychiatric consequences of this disaster using the National Institute of Mental Health (NIMH) Diagnostic Interview Schedule (DIS). We now examine how these diagnostic outcome measures correlate with perceived threat and, in the case of the Mount St. Helens victims, how these perceptions varied over the course of the disaster. Perceived threat will be compared with objective measures of disaster exposure as defined by property loss and death. We will examine which of these measures, perceived threat or level of disaster exposure, more closely correlates with psychiatric morbidity as measured by the DIS. We also will evaluate the long-term threat posed by this disaster by differentiating the perceived dangers from flooding and volcanic activity. The victims' self-reports of negative and positive health consequences of the disaster will be reviewed and compared with diagnostic outcome measures. Finally, we will examine the role of a number of perceptive and objective variables as potential mediators of the stress response patterns.

LITERATURE REVIEW

In the stress response literature, perception of threat is considered a major factor in a number of conceptual paradigms. Lazarus (1966) has emphasized cognitive appraisal of stressful situations as an important determinant of stress and anxiety reactions. Endler (1975) stressed the importance of perception of threat as a mediator of stress reactions in his person-situation interactional model of anxiety. Spielberger (1972) included perception as an important variable in his state-trait model of anxiety. He defined stress as "transactions between the person and the environment in which stressors are linked to anxiety reactions by the perception of threat" (Speilberger 1979 p. 47). This definition is consistent with the conceptual model used in this study of Mount St. Helens victims.

In this section we will review a number of disaster studies that have addressed issues of perception of threat. These include three studies that dealt with hypothetical disaster situations (Golant and Burton 1969; Sims and Baumann 1972; Simpson-Housley 1978), the Love Canal chemical hazard (Fowlkes and Miller 1982), and a flood in Argentina (Dunal et al. 1985). We focus on three studies that address perceived threat and stress as they relate to the Mount St. Helens disaster (Green et al. 1981; Perry et al. 1982; Leik et al. 1982; Roberts et al. 1981; Roberts and Dillman 1981) and briefly discuss the literature on positive outcomes of stress (Yalom 1980; Maddi 1980; Janis 1962; Taylor 1977).

Golant and Burton (1969) used a semantic differential scale of bipolar adjectives (for example, orderly/chaotic, strong/weak) to assess perceptions of various types of disasters ranging from earthquakes to epidemics (volcanic disasters were not included, however). On the basis of the ratings of 58 subjects, they identified four clusters of adjective pairs, which they labeled stability, controllability, magnitude, and expectancy. Three distinctive groups of hazards—technological, natural, and quasi-natural—also were examined using factor analysis. Respondents' assessments varied considerably for different types of hazards. Sims and Baumann (1972) compared perceptions of control, tornado threat, and coping styles among a small homogeneous sample drawn from a northern and a southern state. Among Southerners, they found a more passive, fatalistic attitude and a lack of trust in and inattention to formal warning systems. They suggested that these factors may be related to maladaptive coping styles, which result in disproportionately higher death rates from tornadoes in the South. Another study, by Simpson-Housley (1978), addressed the relationship between locus of control and perception of earthquake threat. Interviews were conducted with a random sample of 187 residents in a New Zealand community at risk for seismic activity. Those with an internal locus of control perceived greater potential for disruption from an earthquake and were more likely to take preventive actions than those with externally centered control.

Perceptions of threat were the focus of Fowlkes and Miller's (1982) study of Love Canal residents. They conducted semistructured interviews with a random sample of homeowners in the area. They found that beliefs regarding chemical contamination and associated health risks were related to a variety of sociodemographic factors. Younger residents and those with dependent children perceived more widespread chemical contamination than did older homeowners with no dependents. Dunal et al. (1985) studied perceived disruption among a representative sample of Argentine flood victims. Using a retrospective self-assessment scale of perceived disruption, they administered questionnaires one year after the evacuation. A number of factors were associated with higher levels of perceived disruption, including presence of children in the family, employment outside the home, greater perceived danger, early evacuation, high material losses, and lack of assistance in evacuating. Dunal et al. concluded that victims who perceived their situation as traumatic and perceived themselves to be more vulnerable were at greater risk of a heightened sense of distress.

Greene et al. (1981; Perry et al. 1982) focused specifically on perceptions of threat in their study of seven communities near Mount St. Helens during the early eruptive period in March 1980. Using directories for communities that were within a 40 mile radius of the mountain, they drew a probability sample of 230 residents. Brief telephone interviews were conducted with 76 percent of the sample during early April 1980. These investigators found that prior to the tremors, which began in March 1980, most respondents believed that volcanic activity was unlikely to affect their personal safety. After tremors began, area residents became increasingly sensitized to the possibility of eruptive activity. Although awareness of the hazard increased, people had difficulty understanding the nature of the threat. In response to the inquiry, "In what ways will your safety be affected by Mount St. Helens?" 31 percent of respondents said they did not know. Only one respondent out of the total sample mentioned the possibility of an explosive eruption. Most respondents reported that they felt certain that they had adequate information for self-protection, that they received information about the volcanic activity four or more times per day, and that they depended primarily on mass media, television, newspaper, and radio for that information.

These investigators divided respondents into groups according to whether they lived at close, intermediate, or relatively distant locations from the mountain. Ironically, the more distant location, Longview, Washington, subsequently experienced greater impact from the major eruption and continued flood threat. This was due to the particular nature of the Mount St. Helens eruption and the subsequent flood threat that it triggered. Increased silt deposits in rivers leading from the mountain, as well as a potentially unstable natural dam that formed at the mouth of the Toutle River on Spirit Lake, added a long-term flood threat to the disaster. The responses did not show statistically significant differences by geographic distance from the mountain. However, significantly more of those living closest to the mountain received information through direct contact with public officials. Not surprisingly, respondents living in communities on rivers, the two most distant groups, were more likely to identify mudflows or flooding as a potential hazard, whereas those closest to the mountain more frequently mentioned ashfall.

Leik et al. (1982) studied perceived stress in families after the eruption of Mount St. Helens. They conducted random telephone interviews with 152 households drawn from three communities six months after the May 18th eruption. Six months following the initial contacts, they reinterviewed 138 of these subjects. In addition, they conducted face-to-face interviews with 70 families and follow-up interviews with 30 of these. Seventy families participated in a computerized simulation that required family discussion and decision making around a hypothetical eruption situation. The families studied were all two-parent households with one or more teenage children. Life events were used as a measure of general stress, and an unstandardized stress graph was used to measure Mount St. Helens specific stress. In the initial interviews Leik et al. found that higher life event scores were reported to have occurred posteruption. After six months, however, the life event scores were lower. After eliminating items that were seasonally related, the same trend was observed. Perceived threat to health and property was directly related to distance from the volcano.

Responses to the graph of perceived stress peaked at the time of the May 18, 1980, eruption.

Roberts et al. (1981, Roberts and Dillman 1981) studied perceptions of causality and control relating to Mount St. Helens. They conducted a mail survey of 1,489 households living in eastern Washington State during the summer following the major eruption on May 18, 1980. They found that the majority of respondents (83 percent) agreed with a purely fatalistic interpretation of the disaster. Eighteen percent felt that the eruption of the mountain was a sign of "God's displeasure." Most of the subjects (78 percent) felt that they were able to control events that happened to them as a result of the eruption, though 44 percent felt unable to protect themselves from ash fallout. People with good health and high levels of education were less likely to feel unable to control their ashfall exposure. In summary, although most respondents felt that they had no control over the eruption, many felt that they could control their adaption to the disaster aftermath.

Despite the negative consequences of disasters, there may also be positive outcomes to such life-endangering events. Yalom's (1980) work in existential psychotherapy has pointed out the usefulness of dealing with *ultimate concerns* such as death and meaninglessness, which frequently emerge during personal crises. Maddi (1980) has also postulated that confrontations with death and other uncontrollable events can serve as a catalyst for positive reassessment, lending more meaning and direction to life. From the perspective of disaster response theory, Janis (1962) conceptualized perception as important in distinguishing between the real nature of external threat and intrapsychic fears in developing adaptive compromises. In the aftermath of the devastating tornado that struck Xenia, Ohio, in 1974, Taylor (1977) found that victims expressed positive feelings about their disaster experience. Many said they felt more confident in their ability to handle crises and challenges.

In summary, various conceptual models include perception as an important factor in determining stress response. There is evidence that suggests that some types of disasters are perceived as more threatening than others. Perception of threat has been shown to be related to locus of control and cultural and sociodemographic factors. Perceived distress also appears to be associated with sociodemographic factors, material losses, disaster-related assistance, and perceived vulnerability. In the Mount St. Helens disaster, prior to the major eruption, the nature of the hazard threat was not well understood by those living in the area, although most received frequent information about the volcanic activity from the media. Conflicting evidence about the relationship of distance from the volcano and perceived threat was probably due to the specific nature of the Mount St. Helens hazard. Communities very close to the volcano's southern slope were spared all but a light ash dusting, whereas communities a great distance to the east suffered the major ashfall, and those to the west experienced flood and mudflow damage. Therefore, distance was not directly related to threat. Although most residents in the area felt that the eruption was an uncontrollable phenomenon, they did feel capable of efficacious response to the disaster. Such reactions suggest that disaster experience can also have positive consequences.

METHODS

A detailed description of the research design, sampling methods, and overview of the research instrument are presented in Chapter 4 and in earlier publications (Shore et al. 1986a, 1986b). Using criteria obtained from the interview schedule and cross-validated for approximately 80 percent of the cases, subjects were classified by level of exposure to the disaster. Those in the high-exposure group ($n = 138$) had experienced property loss of $5,000 or more or the death of a family member. The low-exposure group ($n = 410$) was composed of residents from the disaster community on the western side of the volcano. The 477 control subjects were from an unaffected comparison community, Estacada, Oregon.

Three psychiatric disorders—generalized anxiety, depression, and posttraumatic stress—have been shown to be associated with the disaster stress response, as reviewed in Chapter 4. These disorders are referred to collectively as the Mount St. Helens (MSH) disorders. Onset rates for the MSH disorders presented in this chapter represent new cases of these diagnoses occurring after the May 18, 1980, eruption and before the interviews that were conducted approximately three and a half years posteruption. Persons with generalized anxiety and/or depression prior to May 18, 1980, were excluded from these tabulations. Posttraumatic stress cases were counted only if the identified stressor was Mount St. Helens. Therefore, by definition they had to occur posteruption.

Perceived danger was measured by a series of questions that asked respondents about how dangerous they felt it was to live where they did at five points in time: before March 1980, when the tremors first began; just prior to the explosive eruption of May 18, 1980; during the day of the major eruption; during the months immediately following the May 18th eruption; and at the time of the interview, approximately three and a half years posteruption. Response options ranged from *extremely dangerous* to *not dangerous*.

Perceived trauma was measured by questions that asked how upsetting the eruptive activity and flooding had been. Responses ranged from *extremely upsetting* to *not upsetting*. Thus, we were able to evaluate the effects of the volcanic activity and flood threat separately. Similar questions were asked about how upsetting the volcanic activity and flooding had been to their families.

Respondents were also asked whether they lived on a floodplain, whether they had flood insurance, and whether or not they felt their insurance was adequate. The interview included questions about evacuation procedures and perceived adequacy of warning in the event of future flooding or volcanic activity. We asked, too, whether the ability of scientists to predict volcanic activity made subjects feel more comfortable about living in the area. Information was gathered on gain or loss of income by respondent or other primary provider as a result of the Mount St. Helens disaster. Respondents also were asked about recovery assistance and their satisfaction with any assistance they had received.

In addition, open-ended questions elicited responses about perceived negative/positive effects on emotional or physical health as
a result of disaster exposure.

We used a variety of statistical analyses, including analysis of
variance (ANOVA), logistic regression, t tests, and the chi-square
goodness-of-fit statistic. In some situations, such as in Figure 1,
both ANOVA and the chi-square test could be used; however, the
latter required collapsing across categories for some of the time
points because of small cell sizes. As a result, the degrees of
freedom varied for some of these tests, and, for notational simplic-
ity, the ANOVA tests for trends were used to report the results of
multiple significance tests. In no case, however, did the statistical
significance of a comparison vary as a function of the test statistic
used.

RESULTS

Perception of Threat

The questions that measured perceived dangerousness of volcanic activity and flooding allowed us to examine the perception of
threat longitudinally. Figure 1 presents the perception of danger
over time for the three exposure groups. Overall, these measures of
perceived danger correlated positively with the objective measure
of impact as defined by the control, low-, and high-exposure
groups. In the exposed groups there was a slight increase after the
initial tremors, followed by a large jump at the time of the major
eruption. Perceived danger remained elevated during the months
immediately following the eruption but subsided to preeruption
levels at the time of the interview. The stability of the low-
perceived-danger score in the control group strengthened its validity as appropriate for comparison. Compared with the control
sample the two exposed groups reported significantly higher perceived danger at all points in time on the basis of one-way
ANOVA (all $Fs \geq 21$; $df = 2$, 1,021; $p < .0001$). Within the exposed sample, scores for the high- and low-exposure groups were
not significantly different prior to the eruption, but the high-

exposure group's perception of danger did become significantly more elevated on the day of the eruption ($\chi^2 = 16.5$; $df = 3$; $p < .001$). This difference in perceived danger persisted until the time of the interview, three and a half years later ($\chi^2 = 17.6$; $df = 3$; $p < .001$). Women in the exposed group also showed significantly higher perception of danger than did men at all points in time (one-way ANOVA, all $Fs \geq 8.3$; $df = 1,546$; $p < .005$).

Among subjects in the exposed community, the level of perceived danger was related to residence on the floodplain. Prior to the May 18, 1980, eruption those living on the floodplain reported perception of threat similar to other area residents, but at the time of the eruption their perceived danger became significantly higher and remained so until the time of the interview (all $Fs \geq 24$; $df = 1, 545$; $p < .001$). The pattern of the perceived danger for each of these groups closely paralleled that shown in Figure 1 for the high- and low-exposure groups. In part, these findings of ele-

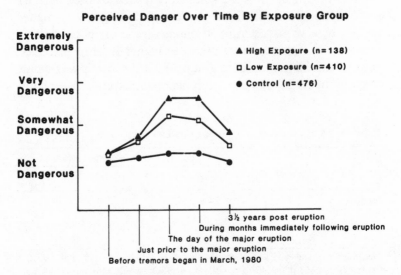

Figure 1. A one-way analysis of variance revealed significant differences between control and exposed groups at all points in time (all $Fs \geq 21$; $dfs = 2$, 1021; $p < .0001$).

vated perceived danger among floodplain residents reflect a larger number of high-exposure subjects in the floodplain subgroup (30 percent versus 22 percent).

Those subjects living on the floodplain also had higher onset rates for the MSH disorders than did nonfloodplain residents. In the high-exposure group, those living on the floodplain had posteruption MSH disorder onset rates of 24.5 percent compared with 18.3 percent for those not living on the floodplain, though these differences were not statistically significant. This finding may, in fact, be a further example of the previously reported dose-response effect (Shore et al. in 1986a, 1986b; also see Chapter 4). There was significantly more ($p = .05$) dollar loss and property damage, but not death, among the group living on the floodplain compared with nonfloodplain residents. Interestingly, however, those experiencing the very highest losses were not living on the floodplain at the time of the interview. We assume this reflects the fact that many of those whose houses were destroyed subsequently relocated out of the floodplain.

Perceived danger also was significantly related to onsets of MSH disorders, as shown in Table 1. Perceived danger was higher among those with posteruption onsets of one or more of these disorders. Women had a significantly higher level of perceived danger than did men in both groups. Table 2 shows posteruption onsets of the MSH disorders as a function of perceived danger and

Table 1. Mean Perceived Danger Score for Exposed Subjects

	Posteruption onset of MSH disorders	
Sex	Yes	No
Male	6.4 ± 2.5	4.1 ± 2.8
N	19	230
Female	7.1 ± 2.8	5.2 ± 3.0
N	35	189

Note. MSH = Mount St. Helens. Main effects for sex ($F = 15.1$; $df = 1, 469$; $p < .001$) and onset group ($F = 23.8$; $df = 1, 469$; $p < .001$) were significant based on two-way ANOVA, no significant interaction. Perceived danger score based on sum of responses to perception of danger over time, questions outlined in Figure 1; 1 = *lowest*, 16 = *highest*. Subjects with preeruption onsets of generalized anxiety or major depression are excluded.

exposure group. Perceived danger scores were divided into three approximately equal groups. As seen in the table, there were no onsets of the MSH disorders among the 9 high-exposure subjects who reported no perceived danger, and there was only one among the 25 subjects in the low-perceived-danger group. For each exposure group, however, we found a consistent pattern of increasing disorders with increasing perceived danger. Using logistic regression analysis, we found both perceived danger ($\chi^2 = 17.5$; $df = 2$; $p < .005$) and exposure group ($\chi^2 = 7.8$; $df = 2$; $p < .025$) to be significantly associated with posteruption onsets.

Perception of the Trauma

Figure 2 shows the posteruption onset pattern for the MSH disorders broken down by sex and level of perceived trauma. Perceived trauma corresponds closely to the more objective measure of MSH disorder incidence rates for both men and women. For any given level of perceived trauma the incidence rates for the MSH disorders were higher for women than for men. These sex differences in incidence rates were even greater before adjusting for perceived trauma. Logistic regression analysis found significant differences between male and female subjects ($\chi^2 = 2.76$; $df = 1$; $p = .05$, one-tailed) and a significant linear trend for perceived

Table 2. Posteruption Onsets of MSH Disorders by Perceived Danger and Exposure Group

| | Exposure group | | | | | |
| | Control | | Low | | High | |
Perceived danger	%	N	%	N	%	N
None	4.7	275	2.7	75	0	9
Low	6.5	108	6.7	120	4.0	25
High	10.8	37	12.1	165	29.1	79

Note. MSH = Mount St. Helens. Perceived danger groups defined to divide subjects into three roughly equal groups overall. Main effects for perceived danger ($\chi^2 = 17.5$; $df = 2$; $p < .005$) and exposure ($\chi^2 = 7.8$; $df = 2$; $p < .025$) based on logistic regression, no significant interaction. Subjects with preeruption onsets of generalized anxiety and depression are excluded from this table.

trauma ($\chi^2 = 16.7$; $df = 1$; $p < .005$). There was no significant interaction.

When evaluated separately, the risk of flooding was reported to be more upsetting than the risk of volcanic activity in both men and women. Among exposed subjects 11.6 percent of men and 21.9 percent of women found the risk of volcanic activity to be *very* or *extremely upsetting*; whereas 18.8 percent of men and 35 percent of women found the risk of flooding to be *very* or *extremely upsetting*.

Respondents were asked whether the volcanic activity and/or flooding had a negative or positive effect on their emotional or

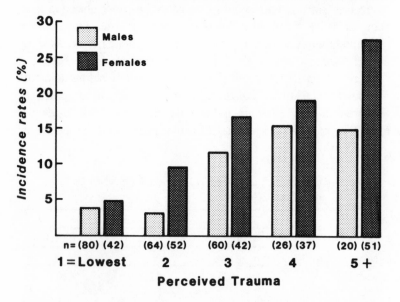

Figure 2. Logistic regression analysis revealed a significant linear relationship between incidence rate and perceived trauma ($\chi^2 = 16.7$; $df = 1$; $p < .005$) and a significant difference for sex ($\chi^2 = 2.76$; $df = 1$; one-tailed $p < .05$). No significant interaction of sex and trauma was found. Subjects who had preeruption onset of generalized anxiety disorder or major depression were excluded.

physical health. For both men and women there was a striking dose-response pattern for reported negative effects across our exposure groups (Figure 3). Again, these results are consistent with those using the more objective measures of outcome provided by the DIS (see Chapter 4). The magnitude of the dose-response effect was greater for perceived trauma than for onsets of the MSH disorders. Respondents' reports of negative effects on their emotional or physical health were significantly related to MSH disorder incidence rates. Among exposed subjects, those reporting a negative impact on their health had a posteruption incidence of MSH disorders of 19.4 percent versus 4.9 percent among those reporting no negative effect ($\chi^2 = 22.9$; $df = 1$; $p < .001$). This relationship was true for both male and female subjects (males, $p < .005$; females, $p < .001$).

Subjects who reported negative effects were asked to specify the type of impact that they had experienced. Table 3 outlines by level

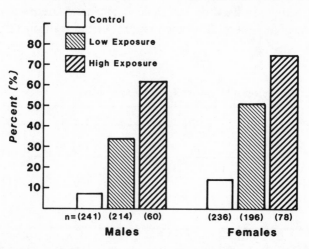

Proportion of Subjects Reporting Negative Effects Due to the Eruption By Level of Exposure and Sex

Figure 3. A chi-square trend analysis revealed significant differences for both men and women. For men, $\chi^2 = 92$, $df = 1$, $p < .0001$; for women, $\chi^2 = 113$, $df = 1$, $p < .0001$.

of exposure the most frequently cited responses to this open-ended question. Worry and anxiety were the most frequently cited problems, followed by physical health problems and depression. Again, a dose-response relationship was present with self-reported negative effects and level of exposure. Among the subset of exposed subjects who had posteruption onsets of one or more of the MSH disorders, 51.9 percent reported "worry, anxiety, or depression" in response to this question. Those reporting negative effects also were asked how long they had experienced these problems. Longer reported duration of problems was significantly related to exposure ($\chi^2 = 110$; $df = 6$; $p < .0001$). Forty-four percent of the high-exposure group and 20 percent of the low-exposure group said that they were still bothered by these problems at the time of the interview. Those with posteruption onsets of depression or Mount St. Helens-related posttraumatic stress disorder were more likely to report that they were still experiencing negative impacts at the time of the interview than were those with generalized anxiety disorder.

Interestingly, those subjects in the high-exposure group were more likely than control or low-exposure subjects to report positive effects to their emotional or physical health as a result of the volcanic activity or flooding (see Table 4). However, there was not a dose-response pattern. Seventeen percent of the control, 12 per-

Table 3. Self-Reported Negative Effects Due to Eruption

	Exposure group		
	Control (%)	Low (%)	High (%)
Negative effect	($N = 477$)	($N = 410$)	($N = 138$)
Worry/anxiety	3	26	36
Physical health problems	5	7	19
Depression	1	5	6
Other	3	4	6
None reported	88	58	33

Note. Differences between groups examined using Pearson's chi-square goodness-of-fit statistic ($\chi^2 = 216$; $df = 8$; $p < .0001$). Respondents were asked, "Considering your personal experience relating to volcanic activity or flooding, would you say that it in any way had a negative effect on your emotional or physical health?" If yes, respondents were asked to specify.

cent of the low-exposure, and 29 percent of the high-exposure groups reported some positive effect. The types of positive effects cited varied markedly across the exposure groups. Victims who experienced the greatest losses more frequently cited increased personal strength and family solidarity and decreased materialism as positive effects of the experience. Subjects in the control community were more likely to mention the interest, excitement, and educational benefits of the disaster.

A double sample of high-exposure households allowed us to compare respondents' self-perceived trauma with their spouses' perception of the impact it had on the family. When comparing husbands' self-reported trauma to their wives' report of trauma to the family, very low concordance was found ($\kappa = .19$). When women's self-reported trauma was compared to their husbands' accounts, concordance was even lower ($\kappa = .02$). In comparing spouses' perception of family trauma to actual MSH disorder onsets, however, considerable agreement was found for both men ($t = 1.79$; $df = 51$; $p = .04$, one-tailed) and women ($t = 1.68$; $df = 45$; $p = .05$, one-tailed). There were no posteruption onsets among spouses of those who reported that the flood threat or volcanic activity were not upsetting to their families.

Table 4. Self-Reported Positive Effects Due to Eruption

	Exposure Group		
Positive effect	Control (%) (N = 477)	Low (%) (N = 410)	High (%) (N = 138)
Increased personal strength	0	2	9
Decreased materialism	0	0	5
Increased family solidarity	0	1	4
Interesting/exciting	7	2	1
Educational value	5	2	1
Other	5	5	9
None	83	88	71

Note. Differences between groups assessed using chi-square goodness-of-fit statistic collapsing across first three rows and second three rows ($\chi^2 = 100$; $df = 4$; $p < .0001$). Respondents were asked, "Considering your personal experience relating to volcanic activity or flooding, would you say that it in any way had a positive effect on your emotional or physical health?" If yes, respondents were asked to specify.

Mediators

A number of potential mediating variables were evaluated to determine if they had an effect on MSH disorder onset rates. Specifically we hypothesized that a number of factors would be associated with decreased psychiatric morbidity. These included recovery assistance, increased income, insurance coverage, confidence in warning systems, familiarity with evacuation procedures, and confidence in scientists' ability to predict volcanic activity. The significance levels for the association of these variables with posteruption onsets of the MSH disorders are presented in Table 5. The strongest association was between level of dissatisfaction with recovery assistance and MSH disorder onsets. Among exposed subjects, those who did not need recovery assistance had lower onset rates compared with those who did need assistance. Among those in need, subjects who were dissatisfied with the assistance they received had double the onset rates of those who were satisfied. Respondents were asked whether they or other household members had experienced a gain or loss in income as a result of Mount St. Helens. No consistent pattern emerged from comparing gain and loss of income with onset rates. In addition,

Table 5.   Potential Mediating Variables—Relation to Mt. St. Helens
             Disorders (Exposed Subjects Only)

	p	
Variable	Males $(N = 250)$	Females $(N = 224)$
Level of dissatisfaction with recovery assistance	.013[a]	.0001
Gain in household income	.34	.75
Adequate flood insurance	.50	.38
Adequate flood warning	.29	.042
Adequate warning of volcanic activity	.075	.41
Knowledge of evacuation routes	.36	.61
More comfortable because of scientist's ability to predict volcanic activity	.50	.28

[a] One-sided significance levels based on chi-square test for trend in binomial proportions. All other significance levels based on one-tailed corrected chi-square statistic. Subjects with preeruption onsets of MSH-disorders excluded from analysis.

victims who felt that they had adequate flood insurance may have experienced less stress, but this was not related to posteruption onsets.

Respondents were also asked if they felt that they would have adequate warning in the event of flooding or volcanic activity. The perception of warning adequacy was not consistently related to MSH disorder onsets. Most respondents felt that they would have adequate warning in the event of either flooding (82 percent) or volcanic activity (74 percent). Most residents in the exposed community (84 percent) also indicated that they knew where to go in the event of evacuation. Again, no significant relationship to onset pattern was found with knowledge of evacuation. We also asked whether scientists' ability to predict volcanic activity made subjects feel more comfortable about living in the area. The majority (57 percent) of respondents indicated that it did. There was no significant relationship to onset patterns, although those who felt confident in the predictive ability had lower incidence rates in both men and women. In summary, for the potential mediating variables that we examined, only dissatisfaction with recovery assistance proved to have a statistically significant association with onsets of the MSH disorders.

DISCUSSION

This chapter focused on issues of perception as they pertain to disaster stress. In conceptualizing *stress* the term is frequently used to refer both to the stress agent and to the stress response (Holroyd and Lazarus 1982). In this analysis we have used an interactional model to examine through the filter of perception both the stressor and the response. By operationally defining the stress agent, or disaster situation, we found a strong correlation between perceived threat and objectively defined levels of exposure to the disaster. We also found a strong relationship between the stress response pattern as measured by the DIS and subjects' self-assessment of their emotional trauma. All measures of perceived threat and trauma demonstrated significant dose-response patterns by level of exposure to the disaster stress. Perceived danger was also significantly correlated with posteruption MSH disorder onsets. Women consistently showed greater vulnerability to the disaster threat than did men, having higher levels of both perceived threat and perceived trauma than their male counterparts.

Although these correlations between perceived and objective measures of the stress agent and the stress response should not be surprising, the internal consistency of our results across a number of dimensions strengthens the validity of our diagnostic findings as presented in Chapter 4 and elsewhere (Shore et al. 1986a, 1986b). First, the pattern of perceived threat over time (Figure 1) conformed with our expectations. The stability of the control group lends credence to its suitability as a comparison community. It also implies that the changes observed over time in the exposed groups were not the result of recall bias. With respect to this issue, it is important to note that our study was characterized to the public as a health survey of Northwest communities, and particular care was taken to avoid labeling our control community as such.

Second, we found a close parallel between our general measures of adverse mental health effects and the more objective criterion-based measures provided by the DIS (Figure 2). This correspondence also held for the duration of adverse health effects. Subjects who experienced posteruption onsets of generalized anxiety only reported shorter duration of negative effects than those with posteruption depression or posttraumatic stress disorder. Higher exposure levels were also related to longer duration of self-reported negative health effects. This corroborates DIS data presented earlier (Shore et al. 1986a). Not surprisingly, the magnitude of the dose-response effect was more pronounced for our *subjective* measures (Figure 3), because the DIS reflects a stricter definition of adverse mental health effects. Finally, the types of positive effects reported by our subjects (Table 4) showed a distinct exposure-related pattern. In particular, 18 percent of the high-exposure subjects reported increased personal strength, decreased materialism, or increased family solidarity as a positive effect compared with fewer than 1 percent in the control group. By contrast, 12 percent of control subjects reported the volcano to be interesting, exciting, or of educational value compared with only 2 percent of the high-exposure-group subjects. These findings are consistent with the results of other previously cited disaster literature (Taylor 1977).

Before the major eruption most of the media attention was focused on residents living south of the volcano near the Cowlitz River and Swift Reservoir. However, the western slope and Toutle River Valley, where our sample was drawn, actually suffered the major damage. Most of the damage to residences occurred from mudflows and flooding, rather than from lava, ashfall, or pyroclastic flows. Ash and silt deposits, combined with a natural dam that formed at the mouth of Spirit Lake after the major eruption, presented an ongoing flood threat to the exposed community. Local newspapers carried headlines about the danger posed by the dam, and the water level in the lake was carefully monitored. Maps outlining the potential flood threat were published in local newspapers as well. Our data are consistent with the observation that media coverage of the flood threat affected the danger perception of area residents. Those who reported that they lived on the floodplain had significantly higher perceived danger posteruption than other area residents. However, since those living on the floodplain also suffered greater damage, these differences in perceived danger may in part reflect differences in initial impact rather than long-term flood threat.

The threat from flooding was considered more upsetting than the volcanic threat. Perceived threat remained elevated in the exposed community long after the major eruption, perhaps reflecting the long-term flood threat. Perception of warning adequacy and evacuation procedures was reported three and a half years after the major eruption and followed extensive efforts by public officials to establish a communitywide warning and evacuation system. Most residents in the exposed community knew about these warning and evacuation systems and were confident in them.

Of the potential mediating variables that we reviewed, only dissatisfaction with recovery assistance was significantly related to MSH disorder onsets. The effects of the disaster exposure may have been so overwhelming that the hypothesized mediating variables did not appreciably offset the trauma. However, we could speculate that without these mediating variables MSH disorder onset rates may have been even higher among exposed subjects. These data must be interpreted with care, however. All of the variables we studied were measured after the fact, and they may not reflect an individual's perceptions or status at the time of the initial eruption. The only significant variable, recovery assistance, is also a proxy measure of exposure; that is, those seriously affected by the disaster were in greater need of assistance and more likely to receive it. Not surprisingly, those who were dissatisfied with the assistance they received had much higher MSH disorder incidence rates both in men and in women. This is consistent with the *disillusionment phase* of disaster response syndrome (Cohen and Ahearn 1980). Victims frequently are heartened by the initial rally of support in the immediate aftermath of a disaster and later became disappointed as the reality of the misfortune begins to sink in. Disaster relief efforts can become convenient scapegoats for frustrations and seldom are able to provide all of the help that is felt to be needed.

Finally, it is important to emphasize that we cannot distinguish cause and effect. Mental health outcome may influence perception of threat instead of vice versa, or both premises may be true. Even if we had measured perception of threat on the day of the eruption, instead of three and a half years later, it would still not be possible to sort out cause and effect with any degree of certainty. However, there is a strong association and, as shown in Table 2, it would appear that perceived threat is more highly associated with mental health outcome than is level of exposure to the hazard.

In conclusion, both perception of threat and perception of trauma demonstrated a strong dose-response relationship with objectively defined level of exposure to the disaster. These findings were consistent with the dose-response pattern of the MSH disorders and further validate those findings. In addition, there were positive outcomes mentioned by those who experienced the disaster. These positive consequences included an increase in family solidarity, a reassessment of life's priorities, and an increase in personal strength.

REFERENCES

Cohen RE, Ahearn FL: Handbook for Mental Health Care of Disaster Victims. Baltimore: Johns Hopkins University Press, 1980

Dunal C, Gavira M, Flaherty J, et al: Perceived disruption and psychological distress among flood victims. Journal of Operational Psychiatry 16(2):9–16, 1985

Endler NS: A person-situation interaction model of anxiety, in Stress and Anxiety [Volume 1]. Edited by Spielberger CD, Saranson IG. Washington, DC, Hemisphere, 1975

Fowlkes MR, Miller PY: Love Canal: The Social Construction of Disaster. Northampton, MA, Smith College, Department of Sociology and Anthropology, 1982

Golant S, Burton I: The meaning of a hazard application of the semantic differential [Working Paper No. 7]. Ontario, University of Toronto, 1969

Green M, Perry R, Lindell M: The March 1980 eruptions of Mount St. Helens: citizens' perceptions of volcano threat. Disasters 5:49–66, 1981

Holroyd KA, Lazarus RS: Stress, coping and somatic adaptation, in Handbook of Stress: Theoretical and Clinical Aspects. Edited by Goldberger L, Breznitz S. New York, Free Press, 1982, pp 21–35

Janis IL: Psychological effects of warnings, in Man and Society in Disaster. Edited by Baker G, Chapman D. New York, Basic Books, 1962

Kates RW: Natural hazard in human ecological perspective: hypotheses and models. Economic Geography 47:438–451, 1977

Lazarus RS: Psychological Stress and the Coping Process. New York, McGraw-Hill, 1966

Leik RK, Leik SA, Ekker R, et al: Under the Threat of Mount St. Helens: A Study of Chronic Family Stress. Minneapolis, MI, Family Study Center, University of Minnesota, 1982

Maddi SR: Developmental value of fear of death. Journal of Mind and Behavior 1:85–92, 1980

Perry RW, Lindell MK, Green MR: Threat perception and public response to volcano hazard. J Soc Psychol 116:199–204, 1982

Roberts ML, Dillman JJ: Summary of results: you and the mountain effects of the May 18th Mount St. Helens eruption: a survey of eastern Washington households. Pullman, WA, Department of Child and Family Studies, Washington State University, 1981

Roberts ML, Dillman, JJ, Mitchell DW: Social-psychological responses to the May 18th eruption of Mount St. Helens: attributions of causality and perception of control. Paper presented at the Pacific Sociological Association, Portland, OR, 1981

Shore JH, Tatum EL, Vollmer WM: Mental health effects of disaster. Am J Public Health 76:76-83, 1986a

Shore JH, Tatum EL, Vollmer WM: Psychiatric reactions to disaster: The Mount St. Helens experience. Am J Psychiatry 143:590-595, 1986b

Simpson-Housley P: Locus of control, repression-sensitization and perception of earthquake hazard [Working Paper No. 36]. Boulder, CO, Natural Hazards Research and Application Information Center, 1978

Sims JH, Baumann DO: The tornado threat: coping styles of the North and South. Science 196:1386–1392, 1972

Spielberger CD: Anxiety as an emotional state, in Anxiety: Current Trends in Theory and Research, vol 1. Edited by Speilberger CD. New York, Academic Press, 1972

Speilberger CD: Understanding Stress and Anxiety. New York, Harper & Row, 1979, p 47

Taylor V: Good news about disaster. Psychology Today 5:93–124, October, 1977

Yalom ID: Existential Psychotherapy. New York, Basic Books, 1980

6

Severe Posttraumatic Stress Syndrome Among Cambodian Refugees: Symptoms, Clinical Course, and Treatment Approaches

J. David Kinzie, M.D.

6

Severe Posttraumatic Stress Syndrome Among Cambodian Refugees: Symptoms, Clinical Course, and Treatment Approaches

Before 1970, Cambodia (Kampuchea) was a small relatively rich Southeast Asian country. Its stable export businesses shipped rice, rubber, and cotton worldwide. The Indochinese war openly spread to Cambodia in 1970, and subsequently the government of Pol Pot controlled Cambodia from 1975 to 1979. Between one and three million of Cambodia's seven million people died under this regime. Hundreds of thousands were executed and others died of starvation and disease in brutal labor camps and during the forced evacuation of towns and cities.

Particularly singled out for execution were Buddhist monks, city dwellers, government officials, and all those with a Western education. This radical revolution not only killed millions but also destroyed the basic fabric of Cambodian culture. Atrocities perpetrated on Cambodia by fellow Cambodians (Hawk 1982) have been termed *auto genocide*. When the Vietnamese invaded the country in 1979 many of the Cambodians escaped. Some came to the United States after being in refugee camps in Thailand for one to three years.

Since 1978 the Department of Psychiatry of the Oregon Health Sciences University has sponsored a weekly Indochinese Refugee Clinic (Kinzie et al. 1980, 1983). In seven years the clinic staff has seen over 450 patients, 20 percent of whom have been Cambodian.

As a result, we have been alerted to the persistent psychiatric syndromes that followed the brutal treatment endured by the survivors of the Pol Pot concentration camps. In this chapter I describe the posttraumatic stress syndrome among adult Cambodian patients, the studies of the children who endured these camps, our one year follow-up data of our original patients, and our suggested treatment approaches. These studies have provided valuable insights about the effects on humans of severe stress.

POSTTRAUMATIC STRESS DISORDER AMONG REFUGEES FROM CAMBODIAN CONCENTRATION CAMPS

During the late 1970s, there were few reports in the Western press of the severe trauma and inhumane conditions of the Pol Pot government. More recently reports of the massive executions, starvation, separation of families, and forced labor during the regime of Pol Pot have been documented in newspapers, books, and television. Some of this was dramatized in a much acclaimed motion picture, *The Killing Fields*.

Originally we were unaware of the severe stress that our Cambodian patients had undergone. As we became aware of the massive trauma they had experienced, we began to systematically review their history and to look for specific posttraumatic stress symptoms (PTSD) using the PTSD section of the Diagnostic Interview Schedule (DIS) (Robbins et al. 1982). This and all subsequent interviews with the refugee patients were done with the assistance of the same Cambodian mental health worker at each visit. These case histories led to the description of 13 patients in our first report (Kinzie et al. 1984). The symptoms were remarkably similar to those of other concentration camp victims, although there were some atypical characteristics.

One unique aspect was the avoidance of thoughts, behavior, and any activities that reminded them of the past. Few had told their stories before and fewer still had described any details. Despite this avoidance, lasting up to three years, it became clear that intrusive thoughts and memories were present that they were trying actively to avoid. The interview itself stimulated further intrusive thoughts. Many patients became hyperactive with exaggerated startle reactions. Sleep disorders and concentration problems were common. The patients seemed to be caught between an avoidance phase and a persistent intrusive phase. Intrusive thoughts occurred during the day and also in their dreams. Their avoidance behavior attempted to consciously push these thoughts out of awareness.

We increased our sample to 19 patients. Their clinical symptoms are shown in Table 1. Particularly interesting in this group of patients was the high rate of depressive symptoms. None had previously sought treatment or even mentioned the symptoms of posttraumatic stress disorder as we know it in Western psychiatry. They did, however, seek treatment for the depression. We were impressed by the universality and similarity of the symptoms that were present in 19 of our first 20 patients. Because it was a patient population we were uncertain how often the symptoms would be found in a nonpatient population. We were fortunate to be able to study a group of Cambodian adolescents who had spent four years in the camps as children.

PSYCHIATRIC EFFECTS OF MASSIVE TRAUMA ON CAMBODIAN CHILDREN

Teachers in a local school became aware of several children who appeared to have startle reactions to common stimuli in their classrooms. After being asked for consultation, we were able to do psychiatric interviews and a home visit and to do academic evaluations on 40 Cambodian adolescents who had been in concentration camps for four years (Kinzie et al. 1986; Sack et al. 1986). Three psychiatrists working with the same Cambodian mental health worker did a semistructured interview that included questions about family life, health, school experiences, and about life in Cambodia before and during the Pol Pot regime, in the refugee camp, and in the United States. Specific questions also were asked about affective, panic, phobic, and anxiety disorders from the Schedule of Affective Disorders and Schizophrenia (SADS; Spitzer and Endicott 1979). The PTSD items were taken from the DIS. A diagnosis was made with Research Diagnostic Criteria (RDC) or criteria from the *Diagnostic and Statistical Manual of Mental Disorders (Third Edition) (DSM-III;* American Psychiatric Association 1980).

The average age of the students was 17 with a range of 14 to 20. There were 25 male and 15 female subjects. At the time of the interview only 11 were with their natural fathers, 20 were with their natural mothers, and 15 were with some siblings. Overall, 26 were living with some family member, and 14 were living in either an American or Cambodian foster home.

A typical childhood could be described as follows: born in 1967, began school in 1973 (age six), terminated school abruptly in 1975 (age 8); confined in concentration camps from 1975 to 1979 (age 12), escaped to Thailand, and became a refugee for about 27 months (age 15). Most refugee students had been attending school in the United States for about two years (age 17). In Cambodia, 36 had lived entirely in age-segregated camps, 33 were separated from their families during that time. All had endured forced labor 15 hours a day for seven days a week. Most had gone without adequate food for long periods. Twenty-seven were starved until they looked like skeletons. Eighteen of the 40 knew that their fathers had died, and 7 knew that their fathers were missing. Eleven

Table 1. Symptoms of Cambodian Posttraumatic Stress Syndrome

Symptoms present in more than 75% of patients
Depressive symptoms with disturbances in sleep, appetite, and concentration
Avoidance of memories or activities and events that arouse memories
Recurrent dreams (nightmares)
Recurrent and intrusive thoughts
Symptoms present in more than 50% of patients
Detachment or estrangement from others (emotional numbing)
Exaggerated startle response
Intensification of symptoms by exposure to events that symbolize or resemble the trauma
Intensification of symptoms with minimal academic, social, or vocational stress
Symptoms present in more than 25% of patients
Family violence, anger, or severe irritability
Guilt or shame about surviving

Note. N = 19. Other symtoms included suicidal thoughts or thoughts about death.

mothers were dead and four were missing. Thirty-two of the 40 lost at least one family member, the average being three dead or missing.

Twenty of the 40 students met *DSM-III* diagnostic criteria for current PTSD and 5 had the diagnosis of major depressive disorder (Table 2). Sixteen others met the diagnosis of some depressive disorder, usually intermittent (RDC criteria); that is, they had some depressive symptoms for much of the time for two years. Depressive symptoms were high in this group, and overall 21 students had some diagnosis for a depressive disorder. Seven had

Table 2. Current Diagnosis ($N = 40$)

Diagnosis	N	%
Posttraumatic stress disorder (*DSM-III*) [a]	20	50
Depressive disorder all types[b]	21	53
Panic disorder	3	8
Generalized anxiety disorder	7	18
Others	2 mild M.R.	
	1 OBS with oppositional personality disorder	
	1 schizoid personality	
Medical	2 blindness of one eye (one also amputation of arm)	
	6 inactive T.B.	
	1 unknown atrophy of leg	

Note. DSM-III = Diagnostic and Statistical Manual (Third Edition). Twenty-seven subjects had at least one diagnosis. There were no cases of schizophrenia, drug or alcohol abuse, antisocial or conduct disorders.

[a] Of the 20 subjects with PTSD, 17 also suffered depressive diagnosis.

[b] These included 5 cases of major depressive disorder, one case of minor depressive disorder, and fifteen cases of intermittent depressive disorder.

Table 3. Presence of Current Psychiatric Diagnosis and Household Composition

	Presence of diagnosis		
Household composition	No	Yes	Total
Lives with a nuclear family member[a]	12	14	26
Lives in Cambodian or American foster family or alone	1	13	14

[a] The relationship holds for natural father, natural mother, or siblings in home, $\chi^2 = 6.31$, $df = 1$, $p < .05$.

anxiety disorder. Twenty-seven students (68 percent) had at least one diagnosis whereas 13 had none. No cases of schizophrenia, drug or alcohol abuse, or antisocial behavior were found.

The amount of trauma or number of family members killed or missing did not correlate with a psychiatric diagnosis. However, 13 of 14 students who lived in a foster home had a diagnosis, while only 14 of 26 of those who lived with a nuclear family member had a diagnosis (Table 3). It was quite clear that living without a nuclear family member greatly increased the risk of having a psychiatric diagnosis. Seven of these students eventually became patients as a result of the study. Although we did not formally examine the parents, our home survey indicated that two thirds of the Cambodian parents who had lived through the Pol Pot years had at least four of the following symptoms: trouble sleeping, trouble concentrating, anxiety, fatigue, irritability, and chronic sadness. It is likely that adults had the same prevalence of PTSD as the children in the study. If the same prevalence of disorders were confirmed in other studies of Cambodians, 50 percent would have PTSD and two thirds would have a major psychiatric diagnosis. This would indeed be an alarming statistic, and it indicates the need for a study on nonpatient Cambodian populations. Follow-up studies of these students are planned to determine the course of symptoms over time.

ONE-YEAR FOLLOW-UP ON POSTTRAUMATIC STRESS DISORDER OF CAMBODIAN PATIENTS

Numerous studies have described delayed and chronic symptoms in posttraumatic stress disorders among combat veterans and prisoners of war (Archibald et al. 1965; Biebe 1975). Depression and anxiety, as well as somatic symptoms have been present in long-term follow-up studies of concentration camp victims (Ostwald and Bittner 1968; Eitinger 1961). A 33-year follow-up study of concentration camp victims in Montreal showed continual symptoms among the Jewish populations. The symptoms increased during heightened tension of community anti-Semitism (Eaton et al. 1982).

Because these reports indicated the persistence of PTSD symptoms, we reviewed our first 13 patients a year after they were originally diagnosed. Twelve of these 13 patients had a repeat interview to detect the presence of PTSD (see Table 4). Ten of the 12 had been regular patients during the year and two had dropped out, although they had a follow-up one year later (Boehnlein et al. 1985). Five of the 12 no longer met the *DSM-III* criteria of PTSD. Three had improved dramatically but still met the criteria, three remained unchanged, and one had worsened. Improvement in these symptoms varied: 10 of the 12 patients had a reduction of nightmares and 10 lost their sense of being on guard. Sleep was improved or returned to normal in 9 patients, 7 patients had a reduction in startle reaction, and 6 had an improvement in concentration. However, other symptoms improved minimally. Only 4 noted improvement in their feelings for people they used to care

Table 4. One-Year Follow-Up of 12 PTSD Patients

N	Change
	Overall improvement
5	Improved, no longer met diagnosis of PTSD
3	Improved
3	Remained unchanged
1	Worsened
	Symptomatic improvement
10[c]	Improved in nightmares
10[a]	Improved in hypervigilance
9[b]	Sleep impaired
7[c]	Reduction in startle reaction
6[c]	Improved in concentration
	Poor response
5[c]	Increased interest in activities
4[a]	Improved in withdrawal
3[c]	Lessened in avoidance of anything reminding them of Cambodia
2[b]	Lessened sense of shame or guilt

Note. PTSD = Posttraumatic stress disorder.
[a] Out of 10 subjects.
[b] Out of 11 subjects.
[c] Out of 12 subjects.

about, and only 5 reported an increased interest in previously enjoyed activities. Three reported a lessening of their avoidance of anything that reminded them of Cambodia. Only 2 felt less shame concerning their survival.

It was clear that patients had improved on the intrusive symptoms, including repetitious thought, nightmares, hyperalertness, and startle reaction. Denial or avoidance state, which included avoidance behavior and emotional numbing, showed less improvement. We were surprised, however, about the degree of clinical improvement, especially in the active intrusive symptoms. The avoidance state may have actually protected against the intrusive thoughts. Our primary treatment approach for that first year included the use of tricyclic antidepressant medication. We felt this to be helpful in the accompanying depression, as well as in the symptoms of nightmares, startle reaction, and intrusive thoughts. Benzodiazepines and propranolol were not effective. Supportive, consistent clinic visits were helpful. It was clear that a long-term commitment for the therapeutic relationship was needed. Therapy directed toward reduction of stress as well as to the patient's complicated social and financial conditions also was important in reducing symptoms.

THERAPEUTIC APPROACHES

Various treatment approaches have been tried with victims of severe trauma. Psychoanalytic psychotherapy as reviewed by Chodoff (1975) and deWind (1971) has been shown to have mixed results; group therapy has been advocated with Vietnam war veterans (Walker and Nash 1981). The chemotherapeutic approach has included the use of amytal, monoamine oxidase inhibitors (MAOIs), antidepressants, antipsychotics, propranolol, and benzodiazepines (Birkhimer et al. 1985). More recently, using the analogy of hyperactivity in the central nervous system and the similarities between PTSD and opiate withdrawal, clonidine has been advocated as a treatment modality. Clonidine, an alpha 2 adrenergic agonist, reduces opiate withdrawal symptoms (van der Kolk et al. 1985; Kolb et al. 1984). Clonidine has also been used to treat obsessive-compulsive disorders (Cumming and Frankel 1985). Because repetitive intrusive thoughts are permanent in PTSD, another rationale is provided for its use.

We now have evaluated 50 Cambodians with PTSD. Of these, 27 have been in therapy for at least six months or more (21 others are continuing in therapy, but for less than six months). We established a relationship in the first visit with a careful, cautious history on current symptoms and remembered past events in Cambodia. This was designed to establish credibility and understanding but not to be overstimulating or too intrusive for the patient. We then reduced outside social and financial stress by helping the refugees contact social agencies that insured housing and regular financial support. A third goal was to establish an ongoing relationship with each patient with the expectation that the illness would be present for a long time, necessitating continued support and contact with the clinic. The sessions, although brief, were supportive and aimed at reducing the current stresses in the patient's life and were designed to carry over similar themes from visit to visit. Because depression is almost universal with dysphoria mood, poor sleep, ahedonia, and poor concentration, tricyclic antidepressants were given to almost all the patients. The usual drug was imipramine, but doxepin and desipramine were also used. Of the 18 patients, 14 had their blood tricyclic antidepressant levels tested. Eleven of these had significant blood levels of the antidepressants, and 9 were in the therapeutic range (that is, more than 180 ng/ml of imipramine plus desipramine). In the last six months we had added clonidine specifically for hyperactivity, startle reaction, and nightmares. Thirteen had started on clonidine and 11 were continuing on this drug, generally with beneficial effects. We were in the process of further evaluating the effects of clonidine on PTSD symptoms.

CASE HISTORIES

Case 1

When originally seen, this patient was a 56-year-old widowed female with a diagnosis of depression as well as posttraumatic stress disorder.

Her major presenting complaints were ongoing intrusive thoughts, emotional numbing, poor concentration, and avoidance of any events remotely resembling the past that would cause intensification of the symptoms. She had nightmares, startle reaction, and insomnia, was hyperalert, and had little interest in her environment. Her past indicated that she had spent four years in forced labor. Her siblings were executed, and her husband died from lack of medical treatment. She was seen in our clinic on a monthly basis; she was started on imipramine and maintained between 50 and 100 mgm. Evaluation after one year of treatment indicated that her hyperalertness, insomnia, and low interest in the environment had ceased entirely. She had marked improvement in quality of nightmares and startle reaction but had no change in her concentration level, sense of shame, and avoidance of the past. She did not meet the diagnosis for PTSD at this time. Her posttraumatic stress syndrome was markedly reduced with the only major symptoms being avoidance and poor concentration. For the past year she had been off medicine but did receive supportive psychotherapy. Her clinical condition remained stable during this time.

Case 2

A 45-year-old widowed, Cambodian female had experienced a severe trauma in Cambodia, and she suffered frequent and severe recurrent dreams of the events. She had a markedly diminished interest in activities and a feeling of estrangement from others around her. She was hyperalert and had exaggerated startle response, sleep disturbance, guilt about surviving, and marked trouble concentrating. She had been a relatively well-to-do person in Cambodia, but when the Pol Pot regime took over, her husband was immediately executed. Subsequently her parents died of starvation, one male child was executed, and another child died of starvation. Twice she was tied to a stake, beaten and tortured, and told that she was going to die. Since coming to the United States in 1982, all of her symptoms had increased. She was pressured by the welfare agency to find work, which greatly increased her symptoms. She had symptoms of both posttraumatic stress syndrome and depressive disorder. She was started on imipramine and later propranolol, 40 mgm twice a day, was added. Because of increased startle reaction and hyperalertness, clonidine was added and the propranolol was stopped. Kept on a daily 100 mgm dose of imipramine, her blood level was 219 ng/ml (imipramine plus desipramine), and she improved markedly. Her children saw the movie *The Killing Fields* and related this to her. Her posttraumatic stress syndrome reoccurred for a few days, but it rapidly subsided. She had a reduction in symptoms for another month until she received news about Cambodia from television and news exposure of renewed fighting between Cambodians and Vietnamese. This greatly increased her symptoms. However, this lasted for only a short time. A combination of imipramine and clonidine, 1 mgm three times a day improved her affect, the startle reaction markedly diminished, and nightmares lessened. She remained vulnerable to stress but made a relatively rapid recovery.

Case 3

On her first clinic visit a 30-year-old widowed female displayed a dramatic dissociative and conversion reaction—she thought she had been invaded by the spirit of her mother. Her history revealed a traumatic past in Cambodia where she had lost her husband, father, and one child. She spent four years doing forced labor. In the United States she avoided any memories of the past. She frequently moved from house to house because something in the neighborhood would remind her of Cambodia. She was always on guard and felt that the past was going to repeat itself. She suffered emotional numbing, social withdrawal, nightmares, insomnia, poor concentration, and shame. Because of her dramatic appearance, the posttraumatic stress was not diagnosed until several months after the conversion reaction responded to psychotherapy and benzodiazepines. She was then started first on doxepin and subsequently on imipramine. Propranolol was added for a short time. Because of increased stress she briefly became suicidal, but this diminished. About a year after the original diagnosis she was markedly improved and did not meet the diagnosis of PTSD. The nightmares, hyperalertness, insomnia, poor concentration, and social withdrawal had ceased entirely. There was still some shame, and startle reaction, low interest, and avoidance of past events did not change at all. A year and a half after the original diagnosis, she lost a job that she enjoyed. Her headaches increased, she was irritable, had bad dreams, startle reaction, and depression. On imipramine she had a blood level of 472 ng/ml and was started on clonidine .1 mg twice daily (bid). She started a training program and did very well clinically. She then started back to work, about two years after the original diagnosis. She found the job immediately stressful. She redeveloped all the symptoms of posttraumatic stress syndrome, including recurrent dreams, feelings of detachment, startle reaction, sleep disorder, memory impairment, and further avoidant behavior. The depressive symptoms became worse and she appeared agitated. At this time she was on 200 mgm of imipramine and clonidine, .2 mg twice daily (bid). Interventions were made to enable her to quit work. Almost immediately there was a reduction in the active symptoms. Some recurrent dreams and startle reactions remained, but she was markedly improved.

These patients illustrate several general principles in the clinical course of Cambodians with PTSD. Similar principles on other psychiatric disorders have been outlined by Strauss et al. (1985). It is clear that there was nonlinearity of the course because the symptoms fluctuated over time. There were clear, identifiable phases in the clinical course with PTSD, a phase with more acute symptoms and periods with less acute but definite problems. There were apparent ceilings; that is, some symptoms that simply remained over the course of time. Finally, there were clear individual–environmental interactions.

We find that severe posttraumatic stress disorder is a chronic disease among this population. It was present for two to three years before it was diagnosed in our patients, and in those we have studied it lasts up to three years. Even in those cases where there was a good response (Case 1), some symptoms such as social withdrawal and avoidance of memories remained. The reduction of the major symptoms of depression and the intrusive phase of PTSD was similar for many patients. The inability to resolve the denial and avoidance phase was a universal feature. The presence or reduction of stress markedly influenced the symptoms. It was clear that the symptoms were often exacerbated by pressures to obtain jobs, attend school, or perform other activities that the patient viewed as extremely stressful and that may have reminded them of their forced labor in Cambodia. Reducing the stress from these sources often caused a reduction in the symptoms.

Some have reported poor results in treating PTSD with tricyclic antidepressants (Birkhimer et al. 1985), whereas others have found them useful (Burstein 1984; Falcon et al. 1985). We found that some of the symptoms of PTSD, including depression, poor sleep, and nightmares, could be reduced with tricyclic antidepressants, especially when they were applied in a therapeutic range. Further reduction, particularly in the hyperalertness, startle reactions, and the intrusive nightmares, had been achieved with clonidine. Even

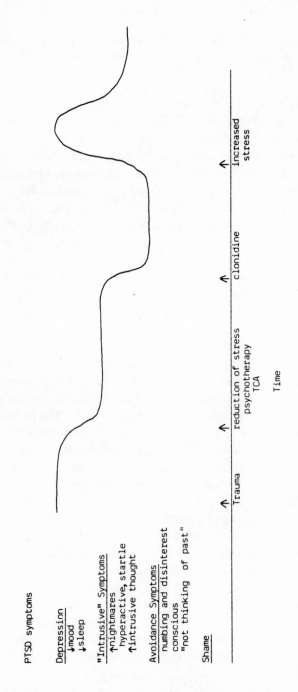

Figure 1. Clinical model of relationship of symptoms and therapy.

so, moderate stress and/or events that stimulated memories could cause the full range of symptoms to reappear, although usually for a reduced time course. Stress included seeing the movie *The Killing Fields*, increased news coverage of news events in Cambodia, and, for one patient, returning to a stressful job.

Theoretical models for the posttraumatic stress disorder have recently been reviewed by Brett and Osteroff (1985). These authors presented a model that describes two aspects of the syndrome, the repetitive phenomena, and the defenses. The imagery is central as a form of repetition of the phenomenon. The defenses involved can be amnesia, numbing, and avoidance behavior.

Our experience leads us to a rather different model. There seems to be a hierarchy of symptoms that wax and wane over the course of the illness, depending on the treatment and the stressors. The depressive symptoms are the most easily treated. The startle reaction, hyperalertness, nightmares, insomnia, and low interest can be treated moderately well. Shame, avoidance behavior, and decreased capacity for work are the most resistant to treatment. Above all, even when the patient is functioning well with few symptoms, there remains a vulnerability to repeated stresses or stimuli that can immediately reactivate the syndrome (Figure 1).

Posttraumatic disorder among these patients is a chronic, relapsing illness with a differential pattern of symptoms. The avoidance, shame, and decreased ability to perform place a constant ceiling on improvement. The vulnerability to further symptoms continuously exists. The work on defining PTSD among Cambodians who have suffered catastrophic stresses lends support to PTSD as a discrete syndrome with a predictable natural history and diagnostic validity. This cross-cultural information can aid in further diagnostic refinement of criteria for PTSD as *DSM-III Revised* is being developed (Green et al. 1985) and in planning more effective treatment methods.

REFERENCES

Archibald HC, Tuddenham RD: Persistent stress reaction after combat: a twenty year follow-up. Arch Gen Psychiatry 12:475–481, 1965

Biebe GH: Follow-up studies of World War II and Korean War prisoners: II. Morbidity, disability, and maladjustments. Am J Epidemiol 101:400-422, 1975

Birkhimer LJ, DeVane CL, Muniz CE: Post-traumatic stress disorder: characteristics and pharmacological response in the veteran population. Compr Psychiatry 26:304-310, 1985

Boehnlein JK, Kinzie JD, Ben R, et al: One-year follow-up study of posttraumatic stress disorder among survivors of Cambodian concentration camps. Am J Psychiatry 142:8, 1985

Brett EA, Ostroff R: Imagery and post-traumatic stress disorder: an overview. Am J Psychiatry 142:417-424, 1985

Burstein A: Treatment of post-traumatic stress disorder with imipramine. Psychosomatics 25:681-687, 1984

Chodoff P: Psychiatric aspects of the Nazi persecution, in American Handbook of Psychiatry 2nd ed, vol. VI. Edited by Asieti S. New York, Basic Books, 1975

Cumming JL, Frankel M: Gilles de la Tourette syndrome and the neurological basis of obsessions and compulsions. Biol Psychiatry 20:1117-1126, 1985

deWind E: Psychotherapy after traumatization caused by persecution. International Psychiatric Clinic 8:93-114, 1971

Eaton WW, Sigal JJ, Weingeldt M: Impairment in holocaust survivors after 33 years: data from an unbiased community sample. Am J Psychiatry 139:773-777, 1982

Eitinger L: Pathology of the concentration camp syndrome. Arch Gen Psychiatry 5:371-379, 1961

Falcon S, Ryan C, Chamberlain K, et al: Tricyclics: possible treatment for post-traumatic stress disorder. J Clin Psychiatry 46:385-388, 1985

Green BL, Lindy JD, Grace MC: Post-traumatic stress disorder toward DSM IV. J Nerv Ment Dis 173:406-411, 1985

Hawk D: The killing of Cambodia. New Republic 187:12–21, 1982

Kinzie JD, Manson S: Five-years' experience with Indochinese refugee psychiatric patients. Journal of Operational Psychiatry 14(2):105–111, 1983

Kinzie JD, Tran KA, Breckenridge A, et al: An Indochinese refugee psychiatric clinic: culturally accepted treatment approaches. Am J Psychiatry 137:1429–1432, 1980

Kinzie JD, Fredrickson RH, Ben R, et al: Post-traumatic stress disorder among survivors of Cambodian concentration camps. Am J Psychiatry 141:645–650, 1984

Kinzie JD, Sack WH, Angell RH, et al: The psychiatric effects of massive trauma on Cambodian children: I. The children. J Am Acad Child Psychiatry 25:370-376, 1986

Kolb LC, Burris BC, Griffith S: Propranolol and clonidine in the treatment of the chronic post-traumatic disorders of war, in Post-Traumatic Stress Disorder: Psychological and Biological Sequelae. Edited by van der Kolk BA. Washington, DC, American Psychiatric Press, 1984

Ostwald P, Bittner E: Life adjustment after severe persecution. Am J Psychiatry 124:1393–1400, 1968

Robins LN, Helzer JE, Craughan J, et al: NIMH Diagnostic Interview Schedule (DIS) Wave II. St. Louis, Washington University School of Medicine, 1982

Sack WH, Angell RH, Kinzie JD, et al: The psychiatric effects of massive trauma on Cambodian children: II. The family, the home and the school. J Am Acad Child Psychiatry 25:377-383, 1986

Spitzer RL, Endicott J: Schedule for Affective Disorders and Schizophrenia–Lifetime Version 3rd ed. New York, Biometric Research, 1979

Strauss JS, Hafez H, Lieberman P, et al: The course of psychiatric disorder, II. longitudinal principles. Am J Psychiatry 142:289-296, 1985

van der Kolk B, Greenberg M, Boyd H, et al: Inescapable shock, neuro-
   transmitters, and addiction to trauma: toward a psychobiology of posttraumatic stress. Biol Psychiatry 20:314–325, 1985

Walker JI, Nash JL: Group therapy in the treatment of Vietnam combat
   veterans. Int J Group Psychother 31:379–389, 1981

Disaster Stress Studies: Conclusions

Mardi J. Horowitz, M.D.

7

Disaster Stress Studies: Conclusions

Having read these six excellent presentations on various types of disaster and various types of response to disaster, readers will wish to draw their own conclusions. To help in this process, I will organize the issues into the following subtopics, and give some of my own perspectives on each:

1. Are stressor life events followed by signs and symptoms of mental disorders?
2. Are disasters followed by particular stress response syndromes such as posttraumatic stress disorder?
3. Do stress response syndromes depend on the amount and type of trauma that has been experienced by a person?
4. Do stress response syndromes depend in any way on the disposition of the subjects?
5. Do stress-response syndromes depend on processes that may occur after trauma and before outcome is assessed?

Are stressor life events followed by signs and symptoms of mental disorders?

There have now been sufficient studies of the aftermath of disasters to conclude that they precipitate signs and symptoms of mental disorders. The questions that remain for research have to do with the nature of symptom formation, the interaction of the perception of the disaster with preexisting psychological, biological, and social factors, and the processes of symptom resolution.

In addition, some less well-studied events may be examined for the degree to which they are comparable to well-studied disasters such as flood, fire, war, and volcanoes. Such events include the news that one has been placed at indefinite risk for premature death from the effects of toxins or radioactivity. These events have less perceptual impact, place the loss and injury in the future, and leave more of a hovering dread than the usual shock of more explosively occurring disasters.

The most common of the Axis I *DSM-III* disorders that may be precipitated by disaster are those characterized by mood states of anxiety and depression. Yet it is important to understand that these diagnoses are made not on the basis of suffering unpleasant emotions such as fear and sadness, but on the basis of feeling out of control and maladaptive functioning as a consequence of prolonged states of mind colored by these emotions. In addition to fear, anxiety, sadness, and despair, which are well represented in this axis of *DSM-III*, there are poststressor states of mind characterized by flooding with anger and guilt emotions that may be equally disturbing. Like the four horsemen of the apocalypse, fear, despair, rage, and guilt follow disaster, and in intense or prolonged forms may lead to the diagnosis of mental disorder. Preexisting conditions such as organic brain syndromes, psychoses, and character neuroses are also seldom helped by trauma, although the person may be roused from withdrawal for a temporary period to respond to threat and may momentarily relish the increased social contacts when a community rallies to face a joint problem.

Are disasters followed by particular stress response syndromes such as posttraumatic stress disorder?

In addition to precipitation of depressive and anxiety ridden syndromes, stressor events may precipitate posttraumatic stress disorders, adjustment reactions, simple but severe bereavement reactions, and pathological grief reactions. Phases of stress response may occur that have both normal but disturbing forms and pathological forms, as indicated in Table 1. The signs and symptoms of the intrusive and denial-avoidance phases listed are given fuller exposition in Tables 2 and 3. Different research studies may combine these signs and symptoms into syndromes, and the diagnostic criteria for PTSD in *DSM-III* is one such system. A useful self-report for such sets of intrusion and avoidance experiences is the Impact of Event scale, which can be linked to a specific stressor life event and can be used to obtain repeated measurements over time (Horowitz et al. 1979; Zilberg et al. 1982).

Table 1. Common Poststress Experiences and Their Pathological Intensification

Common routes of response to serious life events	Pathological intensifications
Event and immediate coping ⟶	Overwhelmed, dazed, confused
↓	
Outcry ⟶	Panic, dissociative reactions, reactive psychoses
↓	
Denial experiences ⟶	Maladaptive avoidances (withdrawal, drug or alcohol abuse, counterphobic frenzy, fugue states)
↓	
Intrusion experiences ⟶	Flooded and impulsive states, despair, impaired work and social functions, compulsive reenactments
↓	
Working through (blocked) ⟶	Anxiety and depressive reactions, physiological disruptions
↓	
Relative completion (not reached) of response ⟶	Inability to work, create, or feel emotions as a distortion of character

Although neurotic-level anxiety and depressive disorders of various types may increase the following traumatic life experiences, there is also a particular stress response syndrome that has been labeled as the posttraumatic stress disorder. In many ways this is the exemplar of stress response syndromes, although there are

Table 2. Symptoms and Signs Related to Denial or Numbing Experiences and Behavior

Symptom or sign
Daze
Selective inattention
Inability to appreciate significance of stimuli
Amnesia (complete or partial)
Inability to visualize memories
Disavowal of meanings of stimuli
Constriction and inflexibility of thought
Presence of fantasies to counteract reality
A sense of numbness or unreality, including detachment and estrangement
Overcontrolled states of mind, including behavioral avoidances
Sleep disturbances (e.g., too little or too much)
Tension-inhibition responses of the autonomic nervous system, with felt sensations such as bowel symptoms, fatigue, and headache
Frantic overactivity to jam attention with stimuli
Withdrawal from ordinary life activities

Table 3. Symptoms and Signs Related to Intrusive Experience and Behavior

Symptom or sign
Hypervigilance, including hypersensitivity to associated events
Startle reactions
Illusions or pseudohallucinations, including sensation of recurrence
Intrusive-repetitive thoughts, images, emotions, and behaviors
Overgeneralization of associations
Inability to concentrate on other topics because of preoccupation with event-related themes
Confusion or thought disruption when thinking about event-related themes
Labile or explosive entry into intensely emotional and undermodulated states of mind
Sleep and dream disturbances, including recurrent dreams
Sensations or symptoms of fight or flight readiness (or of exhaustion from chronic arousal), including tremor, nausea, diarrhea, and sweating (adrenergic, noradrenergic, or histaminic arousals)
Search for lost persons or situations, compulsive repetitions

other syndromes that do not qualify as PTSD as defined in *DSM-III* but are perhaps equally related to issues of stress, as well as responsive to both excessive intrusion and excessive omission into mental experiences of ideas, feelings, memories, and fantasies (Horowitz 1986). The intensification of a normal stress response syndrome into a mental disorder is illustrated in Table 1. These signs and symptoms that may occur during periods of intrusive or denial responses are indicated in Tables 2 and 3. The coherence of symptoms into these phases of intrusions or avoidance-denial has been shown by empirical studies (Horowitz et al. 1979; Zilberg et al. 1982).

Intrusive symptoms are likely to be followed by a kind of secondary anxious response because the individual who experiences such symptoms feels out of control of his or her mental processes. Intrusive repetitions of the event in addition include the emotional responsivity associated with the threat, compounding the anxious response. These anxious responses and the sleep disturbance commonly associated with them may be the leading edge of what the person describes to an interviewer because mood is easier to label than subjective thought experiences such as unbidden recollections, intrusive ideas, and jumbled associations. For this reason, careful questioning about the particulars of the kind of symptoms indicated in Tables 2 and 3 is useful for clinicians who will assess the total picture.

Subjects interviewed during an intrusive phase of a stress response syndrome will be more likely to report many symptoms than those interviewed during a period of denial and emotional numbing. There are also phases of response in terms of different themes. Survivor guilt may be warded off while sadness over loss is intrusive. Themes that are in the denial phase will not lead to intense affect such as anger, guilt, fear, and sadness. These themes may enter an intrusive phase at some later point, even years after the disaster.

Whether or not exposure to a disaster traumatizes an individual has a great deal to do with preexisting personal factors and coexisting social factors. Personal factors involve the matrix of personal meanings, as well as complex variables such as personal developmental level. These are hard to assess in quantitative studies. Yet we must recognize that life events are always combined with internal meanings to create a situation that may or may not traumatize the individual. Disasters draw an enormous emphasis on the external factors, but even so there is still this combination of dual input into the meaning to the self.

Do stress response syndromes depend on the amount and type of trauma that has been experienced by a person?

The types of studies in this monograph present important new information in answering this question. From these and other studies, we now know that the greater the exposure of the individual, the more marked is the effect for the worse, other factors being held constant or otherwise accounted for. As just one recapitulation, Smith et al. reported in Chapter 3 that direct exposure to the disaster (flood, dioxin, radioactive contamination of drinking water) led to higher rates of PTSD diagnosis on the DIS than did indirect exposure or no exposure. Shore, Tatum, and Vollmer (Chapter 4) found that for each sex, high exposure led to more mental disorders related to the Mount St. Helens volcanic eruption. These findings accord with studies of combat related syndromes in times of war.

Do stress response syndromes depend in any way on the disposition of the subjects?

The signs and symptoms of stress response syndromes may occur in a subject regardless of the preexisting level of physical or mental health. Nonetheless, some features of a person may incline them toward higher rates of reporting signs and symptoms of stress after a disaster. There may be a tendency toward increased levels of signs and symptoms in persons who have had very similar yet incompletely mastered stressor events in the past.

Well-mastered events of the same type may convey resilience; poorly integrated events that are warded off in repressed memory rather than assimilated may confer vulnerability.

Women seem to have a higher rate of signs and symptoms of stress response syndromes. In part this may be due to their greater readiness to report such signs and symptoms, as men often seem to feel that it is inappropriate to masculine stoicism or strength to exhibit such "weaknesses." For example, in the study of the Mount St. Helen's disaster (Shore, Tatum, and Vollmer, Chapter 4), female subjects were more frequently labeled as having generalized anxiety disorder, single-episode depressions, and PTSD possibly related to stress exposure. Women had twice the symptom levels as men. This is commensurate with other studies in stress research but, again, may be due in part to social roles and demand characteristics.

Do stress response syndromes depend on processes that may occur after trauma and before outcome is assessed?

Intervening or process variables may be roughly localized as to those that reside within the person and those that reside outside a person. The outside variable most frequently mentioned is that of social support. The inside variable most frequently mentioned is that of styles of coping and defense. In clinical studies it turns out that one of the crucial coping strategies is the degree to which the person will use or abuse his or her social support network. Sometimes after a traumatic event, social supports are available, but the person turns away from them or even demoralizes those who would provide help. At other times the nature of the life event is such that social support is given during an early period; during or soon after the disaster but not later when intrusive phases of stress response syndromes may be entered after an apparent latency period that is actually a time zone of denial and numbing. For this reason social support is a process variable that is by no means readily measured.

The same holds true for coping and defense. Although much has now been added to our knowledge of the effects of disaster on psychological well-being, we still need to improve our operational definitions and theory about coping and defense before the important next steps on intervening process variables can be accomplished.

SUMMARY

Well-conducted research has shown conclusively that disasters can evoke stress response syndromes in some members of exposed populations. As it may be impossible to protect populations from some disasters, we now must find out more about the intervening processes that make a difference in who will respond resiliently and who will exhibit impairment in functions and personal well-being. That will be the location for eventual intervention after a disaster or where protective factors will be established before disasters strike. Careful study of intrapsychic variables such as self-concepts, coping, and defensive styles can only be done with improved theories of classification and explanation in this area, and that is one of the formidable next tasks in the growing field of stress research now that important basic findings have been well established about posttraumatic effects.

REFERENCES

Horowitz MJ: Stress Response Syndromes, 2nd ed. New York, Aronson, 1986

Horowitz MJ, Wilner N, Alvarez W: The Impact of Event scale: a measure of subjective stress. Psychosom Med 41(3):209-218, 1979

Zilberg N, Weiss D, Horowitz MJ: Impact of Event scale: a cross-validation study and some empirical evidence. J Consult Clin Psychol 50:407-414, 1982